"It Is Impossible For Money To Bring You

# Happiness;

The Only Motive That Will Keep Money Coming Is What You Can Do With It To Make The World A Better Place."

*- Robb Thompson*

This book is dedicated

to those both past and present

who were willing to risk their personal reputation

in order to teach the Body of Christ

"The Unconquerable Power Of The Seed."

These pages are riddled with their God-given revelations.

# *Robb Thompson's*
# Ultimate Reference Guide To INCREASE

Everything You Need
To Know To Unlock
The Vault of ABUNDANCE

*The Ultimate Reference Guide to INCREASE*
*Everything You Need to Know To Unlock the Vault of ABUNDANCE*

ISBN 978-1-889723-49-5
Copyright © 2008 by RTI
Robb Thompson International
18500 92nd Avenue
Tinley Park, Illinois 60487

Development: Justin Kane
Editing/Proofreading: Donna Friend
Design: Amanda Fico

*Portions of this book were previously published*
*in earlier books by Robb Thompson.*

*Scripture quotations are taken from the New King James Version*
*(copyright 1982 by Thomas Nelson, Inc) and New Living Translation*
*(copyright 1996 by Tyndale Charitable Trust). All rights reserved.*

*Habits #6-8 on pg.97-98 were taken from <u>How To Retire a Millionaire-*
*9 Habits of the Wealthy</u>, by Michael G. Peterson.*

*All Vintage Wisdom quotations were taken from*
*www.generousgiving.org.*

# Unlocking Heaven's Vault

***THERE IT IS. CAN YOU SEE IT?*** It's the vault containing everything God has for you. On the other side of the huge door to that vault, a life of abundance and prosperity, wisdom, and purpose awaits you. Behind that door is God's over abundant supply of favor and blessings. Can you imagine having access to such a vault but not knowing how to unlock its door?

## Does it seem as if you have been locked out of **Heaven's Vault**?

In an experiment, researchers placed a large fish in the middle of an aquarium with minnows to feed on. The fish fed to his heart's delight.

Then, the researchers placed a glass partition in the tank, dividing it in two. After the pike had eaten all of the minnows on his side of the partition, he could see the other minnows through the glass but he couldn't get to them. He thrashed, he bumped, he bashed his body against the glass partition, but to no avail. He finally formed a belief that it was impossible for him to get to those fish. He stopped trying. Then, the researchers removed the glass partition and allowed the minnows to swim all around him. He could smell them. He could see them. He could feel them. But he believed those fish were no longer available to him—that they were forever locked away from him—that it was impossible for him to win. So he starved to death in the middle of an aquarium full of food.

Everywhere you look, people are starving to death in the middle of aquariums teeming with food. All over the world, people are blinded to the prosperity that God has for them, numb to God's desire to meet their needs and use them to meet the needs of others. This doesn't need to happen to you. There is no question God wants you to open the door to Heaven's vault. This book contains the keys necessary to open that vault and enjoy the abundant life Jesus came to give you and I.

But before you go any farther exploring the many wealthy nuggets throughout this book, let me issue you a...

# WARNING!
## *Wealth In The Absence Of God's Word Is <u>DEADLY</u>.*

You must look first into God's Word, follow the principles of His Kingdom, and (like Abraham) you can say, "Let no man say he has made me rich, but God."

I remember the day I learned about the importance of renewing my mind to the Word of God. Early in my Christian walk, I was challenged by this thought: *When am I really going to believe what God said? When am I going to come to the place where I believe God's promises are true for me?*

That was the moment I made a decision to embrace God's Word, no matter what. That day my life turned around. Before then, the devil could mentally whip me any time he wanted. But that day, I began to replace the devil's thoughts with God's thoughts, which put me on the road to financial freedom.

# *3 Foundational <u>Truths</u> That Govern Your Life*

## 1. All of life revolves around this <u>FACT</u>:

Numbers 23:19 says, "God is not a man, that He should lie, nor a son of man, that He should repent. Has He said, and will He not do? Or has He spoken, and will He not make it good?"

The Bible also tells us in Proverbs 28:25b, "he who trusts in the Lord will prosper."

## 2. The believer's life is powered by this <u>EXERCISE</u>:

Romans 12:2 says, "Don't copy the behavior and customs of this world, but let God transform you into a new person <u>by changing the way you think</u>. Then you will know what God wants you to do, and you will know how good and pleasing and perfect His will really is."

## 3. No <u>DISCIPLINE</u> can replace meditation upon the written Word of God:

One of the greatest challenges that exist in the Body of Christ today is that many (professed believers) are far too miracle-driven or carnally minded. They hope to live from miracle to miracle rather than from faith to faith, wanting a prayer line to conquer their flesh and crazy thoughts that bombard their minds.

Do you know how few people actually get healed at a typical miracle service? Of 20,000 people, an average of 20–50 people might get miraculously healed, representing 0.001 percent of the crowd. That's the likelihood of receiving a miracle through a healing ministry.

A faith that depends on miracles doesn't thrive because God never intended for His child to live on miracles. On the other end of that spectrum is the seeker mentality—it is one of social salvation and a do-good lifestyle. Heaven desires for all of us to live by faith on a continual ascent, going from glory onto a higher glory. God wants us to progressively mature into new spiritual realms—to experience daily growth, excellence, and victory.

— Henry Ward Beecher (1813-87)
American abolitionist and clergyman

## "Watch lest prosperity destroy generosity."

# 4 <u>Principles</u> To Establish God's Word As Your Foundation.

## 1. The Intake Of Bible Doctrine Is The Most Important Thing To A Believer's Life.

The intake of Bible doctrine is the most important habit a believer can cultivate in his or her life. The daily intake of the Word of God is the only thing that will bring accurate understanding to the subject of prosperity. Any increase in life occurs only through prosperity of the mind. When we fill our minds with God's Word, we begin to prosper. Divine prosperity can never happen on the outside until it happens first in our minds.

## 2. Stop Trying To Apply The Word To Your Life, And Begin To Apply Your Life To The Word.

If we merely apply a scripture to a situation when it arises, as we would apply a band-aid to a wound, we can't expect to see growth, change, or mind prosperity beyond our present comfort levels. Instead, we must make our lives conform to the Word of God. It is the only constant that we will ever have in our lives. We must be molded, shaped, and driven by its principles.

In Matthew 16:19, Jesus made a fascinating statement. He said, "And I will give you the keys of the kingdom of heaven..." Notice the phrase, "the keys of the kingdom." He did not say "the keys *to* the kingdom." Why is this significant? I could have the key *to* your house, but that doesn't mean I have the keys *of* your house.

It is true that the key to your house would get me in the front door, but then I might find that every door inside your house was locked. I want more than the key *to* your house—I want the keys *of* your house.

In the same way, Jesus wants you to experience more than just entry into Heaven. He said, "I will give you the keys of the kingdom." In other words, "I want you to experience, in this life, every treasure and promise that is hidden inside My Word!"

Maturity is a growing process that requires your involvement and choice. This may be one of your greatest challenges if you've gone to church your whole life. If you've grown up in the church, you may see the Word of God from a carnal or familiar perspective: "Well, this is just church. This is just what we do at church." You may not understand that your whole life needs to conform to God's Word.

— John Bunyan (1628-88)
English Puritan writer and preacher

# "He who bestows his goods upon the poor shall have as much again, and ten times more."

# "Access

To The Precious Treasures Of God's Word Is Not Given Casually. We Must Apply All That We Are To The Search! We Must Continually Ask, Seek, And Knock. We Must Learn To Love God And To Esteem His Word More Than Anything Else In Life. We Must Pay The Price To Mature."

*- Robb Thompson*

## 3. The Bible Is Not Just Another Book; It Is The Owner's Manual For Life.

Through the Lord's glory and goodness, He has placed in your charge all things that pertain to life and godliness. He's given you all the physical and material blessings you could ever need. By His grace, God has also given you all the spiritual equipment you need to be like Him. However, whether or not you enjoy the benefits God has given you is determined by what you believe about those benefits.

## 4. The Word Of God Is The Greatest Road Map For Our Daily Walk Towards Financial Prosperity.

You have been given God's very great and precious promises so that by those promises you may become a partaker of His divine nature. Those same promises enable you to escape the corrupt lusts of the world and the pressures of carnal desire that hinder your walk with God as well as stop you from fulfilling His purpose for life.

With the confidence born of faith in what God says about you, reject any thought that contradicts the Word. You have made your choice to be transformed by the renewing of your mind. Therefore, every thought, every word, every action, and every circumstance in your life must bow its knee to what Heaven has written!

Dear Reader,

# Before You Begin, Let Me Give You A Few Guidelines To Follow:

- <u>Take</u> <u>your</u> <u>time</u> as you read through this book...

- Use this book as a <u>reference</u> <u>guide</u> to grow in your understanding of God's economy...

- <u>Share</u> what you learn with others...

- Don't believe that by just reading this book you'll see results. <u>Results</u> come after you apply what you learn...

- <u>Enjoy</u> the journey towards financial freedom...

# Table of Contents

| | 1 | The Benchmark Checklist of a Seed God Accepts........13 |
| | 2 | What's God's Appraisal of Prosperity?........................33 |
| | 3 | Understanding God's Purpose for Wealth....................41 |
| | 4 | Conventional Mistakes People Make............................55 |
| | 5 | Disciplined Decisions = Prime Prosperity....................67 |
| | 6 | Basis Points of "Real" Millionaires..............................87 |
| | 7 | Foundational Laws of Enduring Wealth.......................101 |
| | 8 | Lending Your Mind to What You Believe......................125 |
| | 9 | Investing Time More Effectively..................................145 |
| | 10 | Excellent Returns VS. Mediocre Yields........................157 |
| | 11 | Maximum Rules of Problem Solving............................169 |
| | 12 | Foreclose on Debt – Fast and Forever!.......................185 |
| | 13 | Negotiating an Operative Financial Plan.....................207 |
| | 14 | Obedience: Zoning in on God's Abundance.................217 |
| | | "Money Bag" Section....................................................235 |

*Prosperity Confessions*     *Purchasing an Automobile*
*29 Ways to Burn Money*     *8 Tips About Insurance*
*7 Tips to Sell Your Home*     *Insurance You Must Avoid*
*Money Saving Ideas*     *24 Final Reminders*

# "Rich People See Every Dollar As A SEED While The Mentally Impoverished See Everything They Get As Food…"

– Robb Thompson

*Prosperity Pointer*

## Universal Truths Of Increase

### Deuteronomy 1.11
May the Lord, the God of your fathers,
increase you a thousand times and bless you
as He has promised!

### Deuteronomy 6.3
Hear, O Israel, and be careful to obey so that it may go well
with you and that you may increase greatly in a land flowing
with milk and honey, just as the Lord, the God of your fathers,
promised you.

# The Benchmark Checklist Of A SEED God Accepts

# "*GIVING Is The First Step To Prosperity!*"

*— Robb Thompson*

One of my mottos is to: **Live Every Day As Though You Have Something Good To Give!**

I discovered that a lifestyle of generosity was *required* in order for me to go to another level of success in my life.

Generosity is happily giving that which is valuable to another.

It can be money, time, talents, gifts, respect, a helping hand, and so forth.

The philosophy behind this principle is that when you give the same way you would plant a seed, it multiplies and produces a harvest for you. *Your generosity* transports you from where you are to where you need to go. This is a very powerful principle that many of the wealthiest people and most successful corporations have embraced.

When people can't seem to break through in the arena of their finances, it is often because they have never reached a level of focused, sacrificial giving. Instead, they live in the realm of *indiscriminate, convenience* giving: "Let's give a little something to these poor people — they need it."

Many people you know have a scarcity mindset. They tend to hold on to what they have, especially when it comes to their money. Because if they let something go, they are uncertain it will come back into their life. The law of sowing and reaping guarantees that whatever you sow comes back to you in multiplied fashion. Your part is to let go and walk in a greater level of generosity than ever before.

The more you give, the easier it becomes; however, until you practice, it may just be the hardest thing you've ever done. **Focus on one thing as you give — you will reap in due season if you remain diligent.**

The Scriptures promise us that God gives seed to the person who desires to sow. Some may say they have nothing to give, but that is never the case as far as God is concerned.

## *3 Important <u>Questions</u> Every Sower Must Ask*

- *What do I possess that can alter someone's life for the better?*
- *Do I possess something spiritual, emotional, or financial that I can sow?*
- *Where in this situation can I sow a precious seed of a great attitude, a thankful heart, a helping hand, or just being a problem solver?*

### You **<u>ALWAYS</u>** have something you can sow. God would be a liar if you truly had nothing.

Change your mind about how you see your life. Rather than looking for people to solve your problems, find out what you can do to solve theirs. As you do, you'll soon walk in God's abundance. Here is an important truth:

### ABUNDANCE is the reward of the sower, while lack is the consequence of the hoarder.

You must earn before you can give. Share your time and money. Send lots of flowers, candy, e-mails, handwritten cards, teddy bears, and thank yous. Extend a helping hand. Smile. Compliment. Tell jokes. Laugh. Remember names, anniversaries, and birthdays.

# Be GENEROUS
# and then forget it!

Selflessly share your time and money because it is right. You will set in motion a chain of positive actions and reactions. To be unselfish, sharing, generous, bountiful, magnanimous, noble-minded, and gracious is much more about attitude than about money. As much as you give, much more will you receive.

Sowing and reaping is a divine law God established in this universe. As a law, it works repeatedly. For us to live in abundance, however, we must accurately apply the laws of God's Word.

God's Kingdom functions according to principle, not desire. Regardless of what we want, we only receive in proportion to the principles we follow. Receiving God's blessings requires us to comply with God's manner of doing things. His principles produce for anyone who is willing to apply them.

# The secret to our harvest is contained within the law of **Sowing and Reaping**. We faithfully harvest what we faithfully plant.

Fear is the underlying factor keeping many believers from taking the steps toward a life of sowing and expecting a harvest. When Satan uses fear to cause us to withhold our seed, he controls the outcome of our lives. We must face fear head on by sowing in faith, knowing God does not lie. The moment we sow is the moment abundance is scheduled for our future.

Have you ever asked the question,

## "How Do I Give An Offering God Will Accept?"

Well, the Bible does answer that question. Here are

## *6 non-negotiables when it comes to giving:*

1.  **Your Offering Must Be Given WILLINGLY!**
    *(2 Corinthians 8:12, 9:7; Exodus 35:4-5)*

2.  **Your Offering Must Be Given According To WHAT YOU HAVE Without Thought To What You Don't Have.**
    *(2 Corinthians 8:1-2, 12)*

### 3. Your Offering Must Be <u>SIGNIFICANT</u> To You.

*(Mark 12:41-44; Hebrews 4:15)*

Remember this, a seed is not what you sow; a seed is what it costs you to sow. God measures the significance of your offering by how you feel about it. God will consider your offering as noteworthy when you give an amount that you feel is significant.

### 4. Your Offering Must Be Given In <u>FAITH</u> Believing That It Will Be Multiplied Back To You.

*(Hebrews 11:1, 3 AMP)*

You may have been taught it is wrong to expect something in return when you give to God, thinking it is a form of greed. Well, let's examine that teaching. Did you expect forgiveness when you confessed your sins to Christ? Of course you did! Was that greed? In the same way, neglecting to expect a harvest from your seed steals the pleasure God enjoys from blessing you. God's greatest pleasure is to be believed. Expectation is the key ingredient that makes the seed work for us.

# EXPECTATION... Is The Difference Between An Abundant Harvest And A Barren Field!

Whenever we come across a promise of God, we must expect that it will happen in our lives. God is not a respecter of persons. If He did it in the past for His children, He will certainly do it for you. Our faith moves the hand of God. Our obedience to His Word, wrapped in expectation, is what allows Him to move as He desires in our lives. As we sow a seed to meet a need we face, let us expect the promise of God to come to pass for us.

5. **Your Purpose For Future Abundance Must Be In Line With GOD'S WORD And WILL.** *(1 Corinthians 9:7-10; James 4:3)*

*3 immediate things you must do with your harvest:*

A. Tithe.

B. Give offerings.

C. Enjoy a part for yourself.

6. **Your Offering Must Be Given Into A GOOD GROUND** *(Matthew 13:8; 2 Corinthians 8:5 AMP)*

— R.G. LeTourneau (1888-1969)

American inventor

**"I shovel [money] out, and God shovels it back...but God has a bigger shovel!"**

# 9 Facts About The Seed

*1. The* <u>**SEED**</u> *Was Given To Man In Order To Unlock The Hidden Door Of Provision And Abundance.*

*2. God Must Get Finances* <u>**THROUGH**</u> *You Before He Can Ever Get Finances To You.*
*(2 Corinthians 9:10)*

We must be conduits for God's blessings. Solomon tells us, "…those who withhold what is justly due, come to want." Everyone has within them the desire to hoard, the desire to keep, the desire to save. But God tells us that prosperity belongs to those who freely give. The world undoubtedly understands this more than the body of Christ. The principle of giving is taught in self-help seminars all across the nation, yet Christians still hoard.

## Sowing is proof that <u>GREED</u> has been conquered. The moment we prove to God we have conquered greed is the moment God begins to release what He intended for us to have.

He is just waiting for those who will allow Him to distribute His finances freely throughout the earth. Will you be that conduit? I believe you will!

### 3. *Everything In Your Future Will Be* <u>CREATED</u> *By Something In Your Present.*
*(Galatians 6:7)*

> # Whatever you possess in your present is more than enough to create your future.

So, what do you have in your hand? When you let go of what is in your hand, God lets go of what is in His hand. Elijah, a remarkable, Old Testament prophet, understood this principle as much as any other person in all of scripture as he stared into the pallid face of an impoverished peasant woman about to eat her last meal. Her son lie on his bead, shriveled and withered, death only a faint breath away. Broken as a shattered clay pot, she had nowhere to turn. Isn't it interesting that God did not send her a miracle of food, or even give her money, but instead brought an opportunity to sow a seed?

Elijah understood this law and was able to change this woman's life by recapturing her focus and teaching her the principle of sowing and reaping. The seed within her hand was the solution to her life.

And as Joseph and Mary treaded through the town of Bethlehem, God's Seed, planted divinely through His Spirit, was about

to change the world—forever. And the same is true for you and me. The solution to every problem we face lies within the seeds we hold. We must sow what we have if we desire Heaven to deliver what God has.

### 4. The **SEED** You Sow Today Will Produce The Harvest You Reap Tomorrow.
*(2 Corinthians 9:6)*

The law of sowing and reaping persistently governs your entire life, whether or not you realize it! As with any law, you can either work it to your advantage, or experience the consequences it may bring.

# There is an eternal **PURPOSE** behind God's ways. It is not to give us what we want but to produce in us what He wants.

Your seed of today creates your harvest of tomorrow, therefore:

- *What kind of relationships do you desire to attain?*
- *What kind of life would you like to live?*
- *How much money would you like to acquire?*

God tells us, "Whatever a man sows, that shall he reap." So often we erroneously believe that God is going to make our

relationships work, give us a fantastic life, and shower finances on us like a steady drizzle in the middle of spring. But if we are honest with ourselves, we know this is not the case in our personal life. God told Joshua, "You will make your way prosperous and you will have good success if you meditate, speak, and act on My Word." What you sow you certainly reap.

We must always remember, however,

## It is impossible to receive a harvest from a seed that has never been sown.

**Choose to sow your life today!**

5. *The* <u>**MEASURE**</u> *Of The Seed You Scatter Determines The Size Of The Harvest You Reap.*
   *(Luke 6:38)*

The forefathers of the United States of America sowed an abundant seed, going far beyond anyone else's visions and dreams. Following years of late-night wrangling with the Continental Congress, along with the agony of the vicious Revolutionary War, the new government (one designed to honor man's right to worship God) was underway. Its top executive, however, needed a place for him and his family to dwell.

By the year 1800, the "President's House" was completed and occupied. But fourteen short years later, British troops brazenly set ablaze the grand edifice. By the next morning (what many called a "sign" from God), a hurricane with tremendous winds doused the raging flames, saving the great house's shell; the charred skeleton was amazingly harvested, reaped as a symbol of freedom for all.

As you study these principles, you may find yourself in a season of lack in your finances.

## <u>INCREASE</u> is elusive until the moment you choose to become courageous in the arena of generosity.

But remember—without sowing a seed, there can be no harvest to reap. Everyone can give while things are going well. But those who give during the times of struggle, as did America's forefathers, really impress the heart of God. We must establish a plan of giving more to God so He can sequentially begin to release more finances in our lives.

Let me encourage you—continue the flow of giving during times of lack. Do you recall the widow woman who gave two pennies when she had barely anything to give? Jesus favored the widow woman because she gave out of her lack, not her abundance. I encourage you to do the same.

### 6. The <u>SEED</u> You Cast Upon The Waves Of Eternity Will Return Upon The Shores Of This Life.
*(Ecclesiastes 11:1)*

Faith and patience are key factors in the process of sowing seed. Anyone who has been a giver for any length of time understands there is a vital season of waiting between every seed sown and every harvest grown.

One's unwillingness to wait patiently has aborted the harvest of countless seeds. You must be willing to trust God through the seasons of waiting. Israel's shepherds had a choice—they could either sow superior seeds with their neighbors by being careful where their flocks grazed, or they could sow unfavorable seeds by allowing their animals to roam freely upon other people's properties, instead of waiting for suitable lands. Their peers viewed those who were impatient as dishonest.

# Patience **STRENGTHENS** your faith...for it boldly declares that sowing most certainly will produce a harvest.

We must keep up our faith, remain patient, and decisively obey the laws of God concerning sowing and reaping...then our harvest is assured. Friend, never grow weary, for in due time, you shall receive your overflowing harvest.

### 7. *Your Seed Is Your* <u>**PASSPORT**</u> *Into The Future.*

*(Proverbs 11:24)*

You can only act according to what you know. The Word of God plainly tells us, "God's people perish for lack of knowledge…" Many in the body of Christ have been taught that it is wrong to expect a harvest from an offering given to God. To fervently expect something is not greed; it is stable proof that we believe God's Word. In 2 Corinthians 9:6, God said, "…but the one who plants generously will get a generous crop." Those who do not expect a harvest do not understand this Scripture.

In everything we do, we expect a return; but the moment someone talks about money, we no longer feel it is appropriate to eagerly expect a return. When soldiers fight, they fervently expect victory. Remember:

# God's happiest moment is when He is <u>**BELIEVED**</u>; His greatest disappointment is when He is <u>**DOUBTED**</u>.

You see, with almost every instruction, God subsequently follows it with a promise. Why? Because He created us to be reward oriented, understanding our intrinsic desire to excel, our intense desire to produce, and our natural desire for more. He put that yearning within us, and gave us the process through the seed, so that we might always attain the desires of our hearts.

### 8. *Everything In Your Life Will Remain A Seed Until You Choose To* <u>SOW</u> *It!*
*(Acts 20:35)*

In recent years, archaeologists have discovered seeds that are thousands of years old. To the surprise of many, when these seeds were planted, they began to grow. We can be assured, therefore, that our seed is entirely dormant until we place it in the proper soil. While the seeds were in storage, they were only seeds. Yet, once they were planted, the seeds "died," but a new plant grew in their place.

Early in His ministry, Jesus informed us that this would happen. Yet, the seeds of our lives remain just that, mere seeds, until we strategically plant them in fertile soil. What seeds are you holding in your hand? What have you been unwilling to release? Take a look around your life. Everything you have is a potential seed, but the only way to receive a harvest is to sow. Be aware, though, that the Scriptures speak of seed, time, and harvest.

## Your harvest takes <u>TIME</u>... prepare to wait.

Rest assured that, just as crops often spring up without the farmer's knowledge or assistance, your seed also grows up and brings you a harvest at the appointed time.

### 9. *A Seed* <u>**NEVER**</u> *Sown Will Produce A Harvest Never Grown.*
*(Galatians 6:9)*

Any farmer knows it is foolish to expect a harvest from seed he never sows. In all of life, there is no such thing as a harvest that did not first begin as a seed. Many today in the body of Christ continually beg God for a harvest, although there was never a time when they ever sowed a seed.

Though diverse in appearance and habits, John the Baptist and Jesus were of the same family, the same seed, planning the same harvest. And it is interesting to note that as John's fundamental ministry was to prepare Israel for Jesus' ministry, so must we prepare for the harvest God so intricately planned.

— Winston Churchill (1874-1965)
British wartime prime minister
and statesman

## "We make a living by what we get; we make a life by what we give."

Never complain to Heaven about a harvest from a seed you have never sown. In fact, even those who sow never need to approach God about their harvest. The law of sowing and reaping is intact. If you sow, you will reap. You don't need to spend many hours in prayer for a harvest.

- *Just sow the seed*
- *Wait in faith*
- *And expect that the harvest will come*

Soon, you will find your harvest coming to the shoreline of your life, sailing upon every wave!

— Martin Luther (1483-1546)
German reformer and theologian

# "I have held many things in my hands, and I have lost them all. But whatever I have placed in God's hands, that I still possess."

"Hell Has A Plan. It Is For You To Believe That God Has Destined Some To Be Rich And Some To Be Poor, And There Is Nothing That Can Be Done About It. It Is A Lie."

- Robb Thompson

*Prosperity Pointer*

# "You Will Always Gain The Greatest Results From The Area That Has Captured Your Focus."

## – Robb Thompson

## Universal Truths Of Increase

### Deuteronomy 8.13
…and when your herds and flocks grow large and your silver and gold increase and all you have is multiplied…

### Deuteronomy 30.16
For I command you today to love the Lord your God, to walk in His ways, and to keep His commands, decrees and laws; then you will live and increase, and the Lord your God will bless you in the land you are entering to possess.

# What's God's Appraisal Of PROSPERITY?

# "Prosperity Is Having More Than Enough Provision To Fulfill What God Requires."

*— Robb Thompson*

In my own life, I had to come to grips with the fact that I must earn any prosperity I desire. In America, it is easy to believe we should be rewarded for simply existing. Many believe you should receive a bonus just for being employed through the end of December. God shows us throughout His Word that He desires for us to prosper. God is our employer, and that is why the apostle Paul encourages us to "work hard and cheerfully at whatever you do, as though you were working for the Lord rather than for people."

Any prosperity we achieve unethically or by cutting corners will be taken away from us. However, if we earn a promotion through hard work and faithfulness, there is no level of financial freedom we will not attain. Begin today to prosper.

# **PROSPERITY** is not a miracle God bestows upon the unsuspecting. God **PROSPERS** all who prepare for it by being willing and obedient.

**Prosperity DEFINED: Webster Vs. God - Let's See Who's Right!**

**WEBSTER:** Pros·per·i·ty, n. [F. prospeériteé, L. prosperitas. See Prosperous.]

The state of being prosperous; advance or gain in anything good or desirable; successful progress in any business or enterprise; attainment of the object desired; good fortune; success; as, commercial prosperity; national prosperity.

## GOD: PROSPERITY Is Having Enough Of God's Provision To Fulfill His Vision That Resides Within You.

# *10 <u>PROOFS</u> That God Wants You To Prosper*

1. **God Wants You To Prosper.**

   *(Psalm 35:27)*

2. **God Promises To Prosper You When You Give.**

   *(Luke 6:38)*

3. **The Church Prospers And You Prosper When You Give.**

   *(Malachi 3:10)*

# God wants you to prosper,
# <u>ABUNDANTLY!</u>

4. **He Gives You His Prosperous Kingdom.**

   *(Luke 12:32)*

5. **He Gives You The Good Things The Wicked Want.**

   *(Matthew 6:33)*

6. **He Gives You Everything You Need.**

   *(Philippians 4:19; 1 Timothy 6:17)*

7. **God Gives Your Hands Power To Get Wealth.**

   *(Deuteronomy 8:18)*

8. **God Gives You Ways To Prosper (Witty Inventions).**

   *(Proverbs 8:12)*

9. **God Teaches You How To Make A Profit.**

   *(Proverbs 3:3-5)*

10. **Giving Is The First Step To Godly Prosperity.**

    *(2 Corinthians 9:6-10)*

"God Will **Never** Give You A Future That Makes Him Unnecessary."

— *Robb Thompson*

## *10 LIES Satan Tells About Money*

1. **Money Is <u>NOT</u> Important.**
   *(Romans 10:14-15)*
2. **Money Is <u>EVIL</u>.**
   *(1 Timothy 6:10)*
3. **Money <u>CAN'T</u> Hurt You.**
   *(Matthew 13:22; Proverbs 27:24, 23:5)*

The greatest test any man
will face is the test
of prosperity!

4. **Money <u>GUARANTEES</u> Happiness.**
   *(Ecclesiastes 5:10, 4:8; 1 John 5:12)*
5. **God <u>DESTINES</u> Christians To Poverty.**
   *(Proverbs 11:24-25, 14:23; Deuteronomy 28:1-15)*
6. **God Is <u>PLEASED</u> With Your Poverty.**
   *(1 Timothy 5:8; Matthew 7:11; Psalm 35:27)*
7. **You <u>CAN'T</u> Change Your Financial Future.**
   *(Proverbs 6:6; Galatians 6:7)*
8. **God <u>DOESN'T</u> Care About Your Consistency Of Giving.**
   *(1 Corinthians 16:2; 2 Corinthians 9:7)*
9. **Money Is <u>NOT</u> To Be Taught About In Church.**
   *(2 Corinthians 8-9)*
10. **<u>DON'T</u> Expect Something Back From Your Giving.**
    *(Numbers 23:19; Luke 6:38; Galatians 6:7; 2 Corinthians 9:6)*

Let me share with you a story about the importance of playing your part.

*A three-year old boy is playing outside in the backyard. He walks to the back screen door and tries to open it, but the door handle is just out of his reach. He can see his father inside on the couch. His father doesn't immediately get up and open the door. His father gives encouragement through the screen door. "You can do it."*

*The child tries over and over again to open the door. In frustration, he begins to cry for help. The father comes over to the screen door and points to a wooden box next to the door. "Get the box and drag it over here." With great effort the boy drags the wooden crate and stands on it to reach the door handle. Then, he reaches his small fingers into the door crack and pries with all his might until the door finally opens wide enough to let him in. He rushes into his father's arms triumphantly. "I did it!" The father smiles. "Well done, my son. I knew you could do it."*

— John Wesley (1703-91)
   English evangelist and
   founder of Methodism

# "I judge all things only by the price they shall gain in eternity."

*Prosperity Pointer*

# "Giving To God What Belongs To Him Guarantees God Giving To Us What Grace Provides."

## – Robb Thompson

## Universal Truths Of Increase

### 1 Chronicles 21.3
But Joab replied, "May the Lord increase the number of His people a hundred times over! But why, my lord, do you want to do this? Are they not all your servants? Why must you cause Israel to sin?"

### Psalm 62.10
Do not trust in extortion or take pride in stolen goods; though your riches increase, do not set your heart on them.

# Understanding God's Purpose For WEALTH

# "Money Is The Vehicle By Which God Finances Bringing The World To Himself."

*– Robb Thompson*

God gave us the power to get wealth so His covenant can be established. He desires His children to walk in abundance so that we can be financially equipped to generously fund the Gospel. Heaven's plan for the Church is to be so well established that the economy does not hinder the advancement of His Kingdom. God intends for His Church to flourish, regardless of the geopolitical temperature.

The covenant God made with Abraham cannot be established until we embrace the fact that God gave us power to generate wealth. **Money is not evil**. We must rid ourselves of that kind of thinking.

—— Anne Frank (1929-45)
Jewish Dutch diarist
during Nazi occupation

## Vintage Wisdom

## "No one has ever become poor by giving."

# On the contrary, not only is money a tool God uses to show His goodness to the world by lavishing His people with worldly possessions, its primary purpose is to **FINANCE** the **GOSPEL**.

When we begin to allow God to express His kindness and generosity through us, we begin to see financial abundance throughout the body of Christ. Money is a seed to be sown, not a possession to be hoarded. Remember, fear hoards while love gives. Choose today to become the greatest sower the Kingdom of God has ever known!

Think about it for a moment. The pop artists of today have no intention of ever funding the Gospel. Hollywood is not interested in giving one dime for the next major evangelistic crusade. If the Gospel of Jesus Christ is ever going to touch the outer parts of the world, we must be the ones to fund it. We can't look to the world for the answer. God has commissioned us to preach the Gospel and therefore has given us specific instructions concerning prosperity and achieving financial freedom.

Financing the Gospel is up to you and me as Christians. If we do not eliminate the debt we are in, we can never fulfill our responsibility of funding the Gospel. This book is not about becoming ultra wealthy or achieving great prosperity so you can purchase a new Mercedes or build a larger home or wear the latest fashions. The motive of getting rid of debt is so that you are free to do God's work - whether that is in the market-place or within the four walls of the Church.

## DEBT IS A CRUEL MASTER! And many Christians

are slaves to this wicked master. I can't even tell you the count-less number of believers I know who have tens of thousands of dollars of debt. And the number is growing. It's not getting any smaller.

We are facing difficult times. We must get out from under the control and bondage of debt and begin to walk in the financial freedom God desires for us. **This freedom doesn't just come be-cause we want it; it comes to those who are willing to fight for it!**

God desires for us to have more than enough finances to take His Gospel to a dying world. I can tell you God giving us more money is not the answer. We have plenty of money. The issue is how we handle and spend our money. Most Americans spend more than they earn. Imagine if you just spend 75% of what you earned. What would you have left over? Abundance, correct? Certainly. The reason we are not walking in the abundant life Jesus came to give us is because we are not following the principles He outlined in His Word.

## *4 Things Heaven <u>Expects</u> Us To Do With Our Money:*

1. Heaven <u>**EXPECTS**</u> us to produce enough money to provide for the needs of our household.

2. Heaven's <u>**WILL**</u> is for us to possess enough money to preach the Gospel around the world.

3. Heaven <u>**DEMANDS**</u> that we have enough money to pay our taxes.

4. Heaven <u>**FOCUSES**</u> on the poor and requires us to have enough money to take care of them.

Heaven's requirements never precede Heaven's provisions.

If enough Christians grasp the principles of biblical economics and apply them in their lives, every church, mission outreach, and Christian television ministry will have enough money to finance the Gospel.

## *So What Happened? Why All This Poverty Mentality?*

Over the ages of Church history, the traditions of men have institutionalized poverty, deceptively turning it into a spiritual virtue. A brief overview of Church tradition will help you understand how the mentality of poverty entered the Church and how it became an accepted doctrine.

For centuries, a particular sect of the Church has considered the practice of taking the vow of poverty as a virtue. This erroneous belief crossed over to become a tradition in many churches. Based on a flawed interpretation of Matthew 8:20 and Matthew 19:21, the early believers and monastic orders often promoted poverty as a virtuous way to obtain right standing with God.

## *Good Intentions, Poor Doctrine...*

St. Thomas Aquinas, the classic theologian, properly argued:

> **"...poverty has no intrinsic goodness." In spite of this, he went on to sing the praises of poverty by saying it "...is good only because it is useful to remove obstacles which stand in the way of the pursuit of spiritual perfection."**[1]

[1](St. Thomas, "Contra Gentiles", III, cxxxiii; Suarez, "Dereligoione", tr. VII, 1. VIII, c. ii, n. 6; Bucceroni, "Inst. theol. mor.", II, 75, n. 31)

Poverty was considered by the Church to be a particularly virtuous lifestyle, especially for a priest, pastor, or missionary to a foreign field. It is worthy to note that Thomas Aquinas and the saints of his day rooted this belief in a selfish inward view. It was their attempt to show themselves more righteous without giving thought to the effect poverty would have on the future funding of world evangelism. This unscriptural view caused them to lose

interest in the part of God's Word that instructs the believer in seedtime and harvest as it pertains to increase in finances.

The <u>Roman Church</u> and the vow of poverty:

> **The Roman Church laid the foundation for poverty that formed the mindset of traditional understanding that now dominates much Christian thinking. This tradition erroneously taught that voluntary poverty, which is the abandonment of everything except the few things that are essential to basic survival, helped a person move toward a state of spiritual perfection.**

This mindset created a fertile breeding ground for the survival and propagation of poverty inside the Church. It actually loosed "a sprit of poverty" - one that is now deceptively cloaked in religious garments and defined as follows:

> **"The renunciation which is essential and strictly required as the abandonment of all that is superfluous, not that it is absolutely necessary to give up the ownership of all property, but a man must be contented with what is necessary of his own use. Then only is there a real detachment, which sufficiently mortifies the love of riches, cuts off luxury and vainglory, and frees from the care for worldly goods. Cupidity, vainglory, and excessive solicitude are, according to St. Thomas, the three obstacles, which riches put in the way of acquiring perfection."[2]**

[2](Summa, II-II, Q. clxxxviii, a. 7)

This unscriptural fixation on perfection, when fully understood, required the renunciation of earthly possessions to be of permanent character. This can be seen by the perpetual vow of poverty, which is still prevalent among many members of the clergy.

> **"He went on to say that the warnings and counsels of Jesus Christ were valuable, even to those who did not vow to a state of perfection. They teach men to moderate their desire for riches and accept cheerfully the loss or deprivation of them; and they inculcate [teach by frequent repetition or admonition] that detachment from the things of this world, which our Lord taught when He said, 'Everyone of you that doth not renounce all that he possesseth, cannot be my disciple'"** (Luke xiv 33).[3]

[3](The Catholic Encyclopedia, Volume XII, Copyright © 1911 by Robert Appleton Company Online Edition Copyright © 1999 by Kevin Knight)

It is hard to understand how the theologians and religious leaders of the past, men of God who were supposed to dedicate themselves to the study of God's Word, could have overlooked such a clear contradiction to the poverty doctrine they were formulating. Not only that, but when Jesus spoke of renouncing all that a person possesses, it wasn't a command to enter a state of poverty. Neither was it an invitation to the clergy to take a vow of poverty. When taken in its proper context, it is the first step toward surrendering ownership of material goods, and acknowledgement that everything you control is the property of God.

Dominican priests also endorsed poverty as a spiritual virtue. Honorious III wrote about these monks in 1217 as:

**"Filled with the fervor of the Spirit and free from the burden of the possessions of the rich, with firm resolve they [the Dominicans] devoted their life to preaching the Gospel. They went about their duties with great humility and lived a life of voluntary poverty, exposing themselves to innumerable dangers and sufferings, for the salvation of others."**

Get a firm hold on this truth. God is not impressed by what we are willing to do without in an attempt to please Him. Instead, the Word of God tells us God is highly impressed with the proper operation of a person's assigned stewardship. Matthew 25 tells us He rewards those who increase and greatly multiply the material goods He entrusts into their hands.

Franciscans and Dominicans:

**Following the examples of St. Francis of Assisi and St. Dominic, many monastic orders and religious groups blindly followed suit and adopted poverty as a virtuous lifestyle.**

To this day, the mistaken notion that the tradition of poverty somehow represents spiritual virtue is still propagated by many churches. Let me now draw your attention to the fact that the doctrine of poverty is not from one particular sect of believers.

Many of the great ministers of churches today embrace and even glorify it.

<u>Martin Luther</u> and <u>John Calvin</u>:

> **Their traditional roots were founded in poverty. Before the Reformation, Martin Luther was an Augustinian monk who was required to live a life of poverty under the strictest of monastic rules. His life consisted of dedicated study of the Scriptures as well as an ongoing practice of sacrificing all material possessions. With the reformation, Luther left the monastic lifestyle. However, much of the poverty mindset of his earlier religious training remained firmly entrenched in his thinking. In that same way, John Calvin began his reforming work with the religious mindset of his early training in the poverty doctrine.**

As surprising as it may seem, it was <u>Charles Spurgeon</u>, one of the great pastors of the 19th century, who made the following declaration:

> **"Oh! may God send us poverty; may God send us lack of means, and take away our power of speech if it must be, and help us only to stammer, if we may only thus get the blessing. Oh! I crave to be useful to souls, and all the rest may go where it will. And each church must crave the same. "Not by might, nor by power, but by My Spirit, saith the Lord." Instead of despising the day of small**

things, we ought to be encouraged. It is by the small things that God seems to work, but the great things He does not often use. He won't have Gideon's great host-let them go to their homes-let the mass of them go. Bring them down to the water: pick out only the men that lap, and then there is a very few...Never mind your feebleness, brethren, your fewness, your poverty, your want of ability. Throw your souls into God's cause, pray mightily, lay hold on the gates of heaven, stir heaven and earth, rather than be defeated in winning souls, and you will see results that will astonish you yet. "Who hath despised the day of small things?"[4]

[4](Published on Thursday, December 9th, 1915. Delivered by C. H. Spurgeon, At the Metropolitan Tabernacle, Newington on Lord's-day Evening, 27th, August 1871.)

Let there be no misunderstanding. God most certainly uses small things. However, this in no way changes His desire to do things in a big way. God does not have to deprive us of the good things of life in order to use us in His great harvest of souls.

In his sermon, <u>Jonathon Edwards</u> said:

"The Excellency of Christ," Jonathon Edwards (1703-1758), the great preacher of the first Great Awakening preached that Jesus chose to live in poverty. "...contentedly living in the family of Joseph the carpenter, and Mary his mother, of thirty years together, and

**afterwards choosing outward meanness, poverty, and contempt, rather than earthly greatness: in his washing his disciples' feet, and in all his speeches and deportment towards them."**

Another Great Awakening revivalist, <u>Charles Finney</u>, in the mid-1900s, remarked,

**"...dwell much upon your temporal and spiritual good things, and spend much time in blessing and thanking God for existence, life, health, sickness, poverty, or wealth or whatever his providence has allotted you–that you were born in this age–in this land–under such circumstances..."**

Many of these great men from the past were mightily used of God and did much to further the Gospel. They deserve our respect and our thanks. These quotations are simply examples of how famous Christian leaders have the ability to release, preserve, and propagate an unscriptural doctrine in the Church.

"It Is Impossible For Money To Do Little More Than Reveal Who **You** Already Are."

- *Robb Thompson*

Prosperity Pointer

# "The Habit Of Managing Money Is Much More Important Than The Amount You Must Learn To Manage."

## – Robb Thompson

## Universal Truths Of Increase

### Psalm 144.13
Our barns will be filled with every kind of provision.
Our sheep will increase by thousands,
by tens of thousands in our fields...

### Jeremiah 23.3
But I will gather together the remnant of my flock from
wherever I have driven them. I will bring them back into their
own fold, and they will be fruitful and increase in number.

# Conventional
# MISTAKES
# People Make

# "The Wealthy Learn From Others' Mistakes, While Those Without Don't Even Learn From Their Own."

*— Robb Thompson*

When someone says, "Financial Freedom," what comes to your mind? Is it fear, excitement, hopelessness?

Did you know that 60% of all families have so little in the way of savings that they can only sustain their lifestyle for about 30 days if they lose their jobs? -

What would you guess when asked how many on average save 10% of their income?
- How about 5%?
- How about 3%?
- **The actual answer is less than 2%.**

**Take a look at these striking statistics...**
- About 43% of American families spend more than they earn each year.

- Average households carry some $8,000 in credit card debt.
- Personal bankruptcies have doubled in the past decade.

It's not clear exactly where the debt trend will take U.S. consumers or the U.S. economy. But it is clear that both are sailing in uncharted waters.

American consumers owe a grand total of $2.5 trillion according to the latest statistics on consumer credit from the federal reserve. That's about $18,654 per household, a figure that doesn't include mortgage debt. The number is up more than 41% from the $1.3999 trillion consumers owed in 1998.

## *4-Step <u>Reality</u> <u>Check</u> To See Where You "Really" Stand Financially.*

### Step 1: Calculate (or estimate) lifetime earnings.
Go back over your working adult life and total up all the income you have earned.

### Step 2: Add together your savings and assets.
Use the market value of your assets, not what you paid for them. If you own a home, then you can only use the amount of the equity that you have in your home. The bank's share (mortgage) is not your asset, it's your liability or debt.

### Step 3: Subtract any unsecured debts (i.e., credit card debt) from your assets.

**Step 4: Divide the number in step 1 by the number in step 3.**
What percentage of your total earnings do you still have? If, after earning all the money you have in your lifetime, you have debt and no savings, what does that say about your handling of money?

One of your primary responsibilities to God and to the people in your life is for you to achieve financial freedom, to reach the point where you can be a distributor of wealth for God's Kingdom.

Financial freedom is achieved many ways. But God's Word must be your foundation and motivation. Here is a simple and practical way to becoming financially free. If you saved $100 per month every year from the ages of 20 to 65, and you invested that money in a well-managed mutual fund in the American stock market, you would earn an average of 10.8% per annum on your investment. At that rate, you would have more than $1,200,000 when you retired.

One stipulation: **We must do it God's way!**

Why is it then that everybody does not become financially FREE over the course of his or her working lifetime?

## 12 Reasons Why <u>95%</u> Of People Do Not Achieve Financial Freedom!

**Reason #1 – Have Yet To Define For Themselves What Financial Freedom Means To Them.**

# Financial freedom is the ability to do what <u>GOD</u> requires of you.

**Reason #2 – Do Not Believe Financial Freedom Is Possible** *(maybe for others, but not themselves).*

**Reason #3 – Don't Believe Financial Freedom Is God's Will.**

**Reason #4 – Consistently Abuse The 5 Core Laws Of Money.**

1. **Law of sowing & reaping:** what you sow you will reap.

2. **Law of value:** add more value; earn more money.

3. **Law of compound interest:** money grows exponentially over time.

4. **Law of problem solving:** the greater the problems you solve the greater the rewards you receive.

5. **Law of attraction:** you attract who you are, not what you want.

**Reason #5 – Desire Instant Wealth.**

You can't build anything short term. Over 85% of people who inherit money or win the lottery lose it within 2 years.

**Reason #6 – Do Not Have A Realistic Financial Plan.**

**Reason #7 – Do Not Follow Through On Their Plan.**

Most people give up when it gets too hard or when they suffer a financial loss.

**Reason #8 – Compromise Their Integrity For Financial Gain.**

**Reason #9 – Put Their Trust In Money.**

**Reason #10 – Don't Honor Their Parents.**

When I speak of prosperity, I do not only confine it to money. Money, you see, has only a small role to play on the diverse stage of prosperity. What I refer to is a full and abundant life. God has told humanity for more than four thousand years to honor their parents. And God promises a long, full life of blessings to those who do.

# Remember!
## Man looks at the outward actions, but God looks on our <u>HEART</u>.

There are many people who do not have Godly parents. Nevertheless, the Scriptures do not exempt such people from honoring their parents. You can honor those who don't know the Lord just as you can those who do. Unsaved parents can be won to the Lord through honor.

We owe it to them; maybe not for what they did or who they are, but because of what God did. We must begin today to honor our parents. Take some time to think about what you can do to show honor towards them. I guarantee it will make a huge difference in their lives, and you will be blessed for doing so.

**Reason #11 – Overlook The Power Of The Tithe** *(10% of your income).*

**Reason #12 – Never Get Quality Personal Coaching.**

## *3 Great <u>Reasons</u> To Hire A Personal Life Coach:*

*1. Maintain focus.*
*2. Personal accountability.*
*3. Measurable results.*

You can check out my personal coaching program on my website at **www.robbthompson.com**.

# 10 Surefire <u>Directives</u> To Financial Freedom:

1. **Determine Your Financial Values.**
2. **Posture As A Student And Lifetime Learner.** *Pursue and learn from those who are financially free.*
3. **Set Clear Financial Goals.** *How much do you want to earn 5 years from now?*
4. **Read Financial Books.** *The one you are reading now will do!*
5. **Break Parkinson's Law** *(Expenditures Invariably Rise To Meet Income).*
6. **Learn Money Management Skills.**
7. **Develop The Habits That Will Make You Wealthy** *(Chapter 6).*
8. **Take Action Every Day That Will Move You One Step Closer To Financial Freedom.**
9. **Carefully Evaluate Expenditures Before You Make Them.**
10. **Be Sure To Take Immediate Action On Your Plans.** *Each step you take, no matter how small, gets you closer to your goals and aspirations.*

# 23 Practical <u>Pitfalls</u> That Must Be Avoided

No matter how dedicated you are to bettering your finances, some things can hinder you. I call them pitfalls. Most people learn to avoid them only after suffering loss because of them.

1. **Early payoff restrictions** – Usually found in the small print of some loan contracts. Intended to keep the borrower from repaying the loan before the due date.

2. **Prepaid interest** – Sometimes called "add-on interest." Pre-calculated so that it must all be paid, even if you pay off the loan early.

3. **Leasing an automobile** – A definite pitfall to the average person. There is no down payment, but you, who pay all the money, never own the car.

4. **Passbook savings** – The standard savings account most banks offer. Usually pays the lowest interest. Ask about CD, money-market, and other high-yield accounts.

5. **Door-to-door sales** – A few fine companies sell their products door to door, but many items sold this way are no bargain. Always comparison shop at retail or wholesale stores.

6. **Seasonal recreational equipment** – Usually very costly to buy, store, maintain, and insure, and it goes unused most of the year.

7. **Cosigning a loan** – A cosigner promises to pay a loan if the borrower cannot. The Bible warns, "It is poor judgment to countersign another's note, to become responsible for his debts" *(Proverbs 17:18, TLB).*

8. **Dealer extras** – Items and services offered at extra cost by a new car dealer.

9. **Home mortgage insurance** – Usually you can buy far less costly term insurance to pay off your home.

10. **Zero deductible insurance** – Pays in full on comprehensive or health policies. Drastically raises your premium.

11. **Non-interest-bearing deposits** – For utilities, mortgage escrow accounts, automobiles, home improvements, etc. Keep these to an absolute minimum.

12. **Lending** – Lend if you want to, but be very careful. Never lend anyone more than you are ready to give them.

13. **Setting fashion trends** – Get ready to pay big money!

14. **Top of the line** – Pay more for quality, time saved, and convenience, not a cosmetic job on a basic unit.

15. **Credit card installments** – Almost any kind of loan is cheaper. Never make minimum payments.

16. **Uncapped variable interest rates** – Always be cautious of variable interest rate loans. Reject any loan that has no rate cap.

17. **Convenience-store grocery shopping** – If you shop only this way, you pay a lot for convenience. Prices run higher and sizes are smaller than at supermarkets or discounters.

18. **Daily grocery shopping** – Buying groceries a meal at a time can cost double or triple what shopping for a whole week at once would. Plan menus ahead.

19. **No grocery list shopping** – Always have a well-planned list. Write daily menus and list ingredients for each meal.

20. **Grocery shopping when hungry** – Never do it. You will buy things you otherwise never would.

21. **Shopping in unfamiliar stores** – It takes more time and makes you less aware of price differences.

22. **Full-fare airline tickets** – Plan and book air trips well ahead. Fares may be up to 80 percent lower.

23. **Non-assumption clauses in home loans** – Always try to have clauses dropped keeping a new owner from assuming your loan before you sign. Such a clause may hinder you when you go to sell.

— Robert Murray McCheyne (1813-43)
Scottish pastor

## "There are many hearing me who now know well that they are not Christians because they do not love to give. To give largely and liberally, not grudging at all, requires a new heart."

# "Our Decisions, Not The Conditions Of Our Lives, Determine Our Destiny."

## *– Robb Thompson*

## Universal Truths Of Increase

### *Proverbs 11.24-25*
There is one who scatters, yet increases more; and there is one who withholds more than is right, but it leads to poverty. The generous soul will be made rich, and he who waters will also be watered himself.

### *Matthew 19.29*
And everyone who has left houses or brothers or sisters or father or mother or wife or children or lands, for My name's sake, shall receive a hundredfold, and inherit eternal life.

# Disciplined
## DECISIONS
# =
# Prime
# Prosperity

# "Our Circumstances Of Today Are Photocopies Of Decisions We Made Yesterday."

### – Robb Thompson

Different choices take you down different paths. Wrong choices take you to places you don't want to go. Or you can choose *on purpose* to become everything you were destined to become!

## Life is built by choices, not by a series of chance occurrences.

Yes, that choice involves a great deal of change, which isn't always easy. But once you become willing to do whatever it takes to win at life, *nothing* can hold you back — not vain pressures, nor another person's criticisms, nor any adverse circumstances assigned to trap you in the mire of mediocrity.

# In the game of life, principle, not emotion, will decide your fate.

Just how important are the decisions we make? They are the determining factors of the success or failure of our future. **The <u>CHOICES</u> we make today determine who we become tomorrow.**

We make thousands of decisions every day, many of which we don't even think about. Our decisions can alter our life for better or for worse. To create the future God desires in our lives, we must select our decisions by principle, and not by emotion. Without Godly principles, we are like a ship with no one to man the sails. The wind fatefully decides the ship's course.

## Without **<u>PRINCIPLES</u>**, the circumstances of life have complete control over our destiny.

For example, many people do not tithe because they are in debt and cannot afford to give God ten percent. They claim that when things get better, they will tithe. God assures us things

will not get better for them until they tithe. Another example is a teenager who promises to stop partying when he gets out of high school. Unfortunately, things only worsen for that young person in the meantime, making it almost impossible to escape the party scene later in life.

We must never make decisions based upon present circumstances, but rather on the ultimate outcome we desire. Whatever we find in the Word of God, we must embrace as truth and apply our lives to it.

 The harvest of your future is hidden in your choices of today.

It's one thing to make a mistake. It's another to make a wrong choice. Mistakes can be forgiven, but we must live with the consequences of our choices.

**Consider this:** More than 90 percent of the people with whom you work every day do not like their job. Consequently, they have a poor attitude, and REFUSE to make the choice to change their attitude. All they want to do is get someone to listen to their long list of complaints, which usually includes the following:

- *They are always "misunderstood" for some reason.*

- *They are under compensated.*

- *No one encourages or edifies them on the job.*

- *They never receive any benefit from their job –
  and it's entirely their employer's fault.*

I don't believe any of these statements are true. Everyone has a free will, so why do these people allow their lives and their attitudes to be determined by someone else at their jobs? Why should other people determine whether or not they're happy with their work?

The truth is, the outcome of our lives is based on the decisions we make. We can actually choose our own consequences. Therefore, we cannot blame our unhappiness or our bad attitudes on others.

I no longer think only from the perspective of whether or not a decision is right or wrong. Now, I always take the time to evaluate what kind of consequences will result from the decision I am about to make. Before any decision, answer this question, *"What is going to happen if I do this?"*

Learn to live with a long-term perspective. In other words, choose to pay the price now to enjoy the greatest benefits *later*. Embrace the *short-term pain* in order to enjoy *long-term pleasure*.

When we make a major decision that gives us nothing but immediate, short-term gratification, we will likely pay for that decision for the rest of our lives. One wrong decision could start us down a road that leaves us marred and scarred in the end.

That is why it is so important for us to understand that our lives are completely determined by the choices we make; those decisions have predetermined outcomes.

For instance, suppose we get up tomorrow morning and decide we don't want to have a good day.

**THAT IS OUR CHOICE** — but we better be ready for our employer to say, **"You need to pick up your severance check because we don't need you anymore!"**

We shouldn't wonder, "Why did this happen to me?"

# Our Decisions, Not The Conditions Of Our Lives, Determine Our Destiny.

Think for a moment about your life and the decisions you have made…

- *Where did those decisions take you?*

- *Do you wish you would have made different decisions?*

- *How does one ever begin to change their choices?*

Well, it is largely determined by one's outlook or perspective on life. **The way you think about yourself and the world in which you live is key to your success.**

One of the greatest truths ever written was penned by King Solomon. He stated, "For as he thinks in his heart, so is he..."

# You must choose today how you will respond tomorrow.

It doesn't matter if other people see you as a success. How do you see yourself? You will never obtain God's will in your life until you see yourself as God sees you. As you change the way you think, your actions automatically follow. Case in point: The reason so few people explored the New World was because they erroneously believed the earth was flat. Why would you take the time to explore if you believed the earth was flat? You see, their beliefs governed their actions. But there was a man who believed otherwise, and his actions followed suit. That man gallantly discovered the New World because he believed beyond all doubt the earth indeed was round.

# Choices are the only witnesses summoned to appear in the courtroom of consequence.

- *Should I go to church tonight in this pouring rain, or just stay home and relax?*

- *Although this book has a lot of curse words, should I read it anyway?*

- *Even though God's Spirit is prompting me to turn off the television, another thirty minutes or so wouldn't hurt, would it?*

One of the greatest gifts anyone could ever receive is the power to choose. God graciously granted us the power of choice. Whether it is prosperous or disastrous, the choice is ours. The apostle Paul encourages us with these words, "For God is working in you, giving you the desire to obey Him and the power to do what pleases Him."

God doesn't just leave us as orphans to fend for ourselves. He knows there is a devil out there whose desire is to lure us into wrong choices. Satan knows that if he can convince us to make just one mistake, it may cause a lifetime of consequences. We can see throughout the Scriptures that God did not predestine our choices. He did, however, predestine our consequences. We are to surrender our lives to the Spirit of God and trust in Him to help us make right choices.

The Holy Spirit is our helper. In Deuteronomy 30:19, God lays it out, "Now listen! Today I am giving you a choice between prosperity and disaster, between life and death…"

# *It is our choice!*

— Henry Ward Beecher (1813-87)
American abolitionist and clergyman

**"A man should fear when he enjoys only the good he does publicly. Is it not, publicity rather than charity, which he loves? Is it not vanity, rather than benevolence, that gives such charities?"**

# You are either a prisoner of your past or a pioneer of your future.

**Every Decision Takes You In A Direction...**

**Every Decision Has A Consequence, Either Good Or Bad...**

**You Do Not Determine Your Destiny...**

**You Determine Your Decisions...**

**Your Decisions Determine Your Destiny!**

## *8 Decisions That Will Lead You Down The Pathway To Prosperity*

### 1. The Decision To Pursue Personal Excellence

*Your Pursuit Of Excellence Is Only Proven By The Attitude With Which You Face The Giant Named "MAINTENANCE."*

Human bodies; homes; businesses; relationships; vehicles; land; our inner spirits; our souls—just about everything needs maintenance! But have you yet realized that maintenance is the key to a prolonged life of victory?

# The largest chasm between the excellent and the average is the willingness to **MAINTAIN**.

All of us must come to recognize that life is won or lost in the details. When details are neglected, they become too over-whelming for any one individual to face. The more the tasks of life are neglected, the larger they become.

Solomon depicts this very cleverly in Proverbs 24:31 when he observes a lazy man who chooses to neglect the maintenance of life. He paints us a picture to illustrate this principle very clearly, "…all overgrown with thorns; its surface was covered with nettles; its stone wall was broken down…" As you can see, the destination of those who neglect to fight the giant named "maintenance" means ultimate ruin in every area of life. Let us allow God to help us as we seek to maintain the details in life that cause us to become one who overcomes in every situation.

**Here is my working definition of excellence:**

**Excellence Is The Attention To Detail That Gives Rise To Superior Performance, Which Leads To Success In Life.**

## *3 Things You <u>Must</u> Remember About Excellence:*

**1) Excellence is a journey, not a destination.**

**2) Today's excellence is tomorrow's mediocrity.**

**3) Your pursuit of excellence awakens the process of transformation.**

**2. The Decision To Accept Personal Responsibility**
*Future Enjoyment Is Hidden In Today's* <u>CHOICES</u>.

It doesn't matter where you've come from or what happened to you. If you want to prosper, it is important to accept responsibility for the outcome of your life. Past issues may have tempered wrong beliefs and forged negative habits, but the <u>power of decision</u> can transform your life.

**3. The Decision To Be Grateful**
*Be* <u>GRATEFUL</u> *For What You Have; Never Be Sad Over What You Don't.*

Perhaps more than any other man in all of Scripture, the psalmst understood gratitude when he wrote, "I will thank You by living as I should." You and I cannot repay God for what He does for us. There is nothing we can do to return all God bestows upon our lives except to be grateful. Gratitude, however, is different than repayment.

# We live for God out of gratitude for what He does for us. **There is no greater expression of <u>GRATITUDE</u> than reverence.**

Our reverence toward God and His Word is not a form of repayment; it is the proof that we recognize we owe Him our very life.

Please carefully consider these three questions:

- *Is it too costly for you to be thankful?*

- *What are the things for which you are thankful?*

- *Like David, why not thank the Lord by living as you should?*

Let me remind you of the words of the apostle Paul, "And so, dear brothers and sisters, I plead with you to give your bodies to God. Let them be a living and holy sacrifice—the kind He will accept. When you think of what He has done for you, is this too much to ask?"

Charles Haddon Spurgeon said,

# "You say, 'If I had a little more, I should be very satisfied.' You make a mistake. If you are not content with what you have, you would not be satisfied if it were doubled."

## 4. The Decision To Develop Sound Character

*It Is* <u>**IMPOSSIBLE**</u> *For Your Life To Produce Anything Beyond The Strength Of Your Moral Fiber.*

### Character Defined

- **Character Is The Values And Principles That Govern Your Decisions. It Is The Mental And Moral Attributes That Define You.**

- **Good Character Refers To Virtue, Self-discipline, And An Honorable Constitution.**

- **Character Denotes Moral Strength.**

Our character is fashioned by every decision we make. Every choice, however insignificant, contains within it a series of consequences.

**There are times when we may make mistakes, stumble, and experience temporary defeat. Nevertheless, we must <u>CHOOSE</u> to rise above those disappointments, get up, brush ourselves off, and move forward.**

Our example must be Jesus, whose character cannot be formed within us except by effort and daily practice. Teaching about such emotional issues as family, humility, and the workplace, Jesus realized that, however difficult, we need to exercise self-discipline and self-control by responding according to principle, not according to emotions.

Circumstances themselves do not determine who we are, nor do they alter our character; it is how we respond that reveals who we really are.

Our lives are a result of the paths we choose to take. Life is a series of choices, not a series of chances. We can only sculpt our character into that of Christ by embracing Godly principles above human emotions.

Let Me Ask You:

- *Which principles define you as a person?*

- *What are the unseen ideals that guide your life?*

- *What are the non-negotiable issues for you as a person, the principles you will not break?*

- *Are your ethics guided by moral principles or by the convenience of the moment?*

- *On a scale of 1-10, what character rating would you give yourself, and why?*

- *What do you need to change in order to achieve a higher rating?*

- *Are you happy with your character? Why or why not?*

**5. The Decision To Link Arms With A Mentor**
*To Achieve* <u>SUCCESS</u> *You Must Follow The Path Of Someone Who Has Already Walked There.*

Beware of the novice spirit that eventually tries to viciously attack each person as they increase in knowledge. Who is this novice spirit? It is the one who thinks they know so much that they rise as high as a New York skyscraper, towering disdainfully above their leader, seeing him or her as stuck in their ways; this person now possesses spotted learning.

Please understand—everyone knows unique things that no one else knows; hence, I may know a few things my authority doesn't, but the servant is never above the master. I have seen many talented protégés commit financial, emotional, and spiritual suicide.

# We must understand that we don't learn much of what our instructors taught us until we are pressed to **DO IT OURSELVES**; only then do we realize how little we knew without them.

You may possess knowledge, but your mentor has experience. Even though a student may know plenty about their chosen field, their mentor has a vast knowledge of types of people, dangerous pitfalls, and real-life situations. A mentor has priceless information and a treasure chest of wisdom. Since history does repeat itself, we don't have time to make the same mistakes as those above us, so we must learn from them.

Are you living as the attentive protégé, or the studied mentor? The Queen of Sheba, though powerful and wealthy, postured herself in the position of an attentive protégé, sitting at the table of King Solomon, becoming teachable and submitted to the wise concepts he learned from the Holy God.

**Carefully choose your posture—it affects the rest of your life.**

## 6. The Decision to Change
*True, Positive Change Is Always A Result Of Personal*
<u>**CHOICE**</u>.

We must choose to change, but before we can do that, we need to know what we want to change.

For instance,

- *How do you go about making positive changes for your future?*

- *How do you know exactly what needs to change?*

Each of us has a certain degree of insight into our own flaws and shortcomings; those we can, and must, change by ourselves. But each of us also has blind spots that are detrimental to our future success if we don't eventually address them. For these, we need the help of those closest to us.

I encourage you to make a practice of asking your closest friends and family members what they would change about you. You may be surprised, or even upset by their answers, but therein rests the key to success. Change. As you open yourself to the suggestions of these individuals who love you, you start taking steps closer to becoming the person you must become.

## 7. Choose A Good Attitude
*You **MUST** Choose Today How You Will Respond Tomorrow.*

If you haven't noticed already, life doesn't always deal us the hand we want. I have three important questions to ask:

- *How will you respond to tomorrow's setbacks?*

- *How will you respond to an adverse situation on the job?*

- *How will you respond to your spouse's poor attitude?*

You're bound to make a bad decision if you wait until the situation arises. Poor decisions are made as a result of inordinate pressure in our lives. For example, you must make a decision tonight to pray tomorrow morning. If you wait until you feel like it, you may never get around to actually doing it. Why allow your flesh to keep you from making the right decisions? Choose today how you will respond tomorrow.

## 8. The Decision To Become A Sower
*Remember, **EVERYTHING** In Life Remains A Seed Until The Moment You Choose To Sow It.*

For more on this subject of sowing, reread Chapter 1 – *The Benchmark Checklist of a Seed God Accepts.*

# "Habits Determine Our Ultimate Success Or Eventual Failure In Life."

## – Robb Thompson

Prosperity Pointer

## Universal Truths Of Increase

### Psalm 115.14
May the Lord make you increase,
both you and your children.

### Psalm 132.17
Here I will increase the power of David;
My anointed one will be a light for My people.

# Basis Points
# Of "Real"
# MILLIONAIRES

# *"Routine And Habit Are The Roads That Lead To Undeniable Prosperity."*

*– Robb Thompson*

Our daily routines are critical to our success. There is a set routine put into place by growers to obtain olives for oil production. Just before the olives are ripe, they are either firmly shaken from the tree or nimbly beaten down from its branches with a light pole, tumbling to the ground like hollow rocks. This habit of harvesting is a familiar Mediterranean sight in September and October when the olives are ready to be crushed for their oil.

## If we create and maintain the <u>RIGHT HABITS</u>, we are propelled toward our dream every step of the way.

On the other hand, if we put the wrong things into our lives, we actually are carried into the wilderness of life, headed toward failure and frustration.

Our daily habits are the avenue by which we accomplish our vision. If you don't have a clear vision of what you want your life to become, how will you know which habits to create? It is impossible. Vision keeps us moving forward, driving us to obtain the reward of accomplishment. Without a clear vision, we become a wandering generality, aimlessly looking for a purpose in life. Let's allow the vision of our lives to prompt us to establish routine responsibilities that are scriptural in nature, in addition to daily habits that are Kingdom-building in purpose.

But you can't create the right habits without a key ingredient.

# Self-discipline Is A Key Ingredient To Creating Habits Needed For Success.

Self-discipline is the most important single quality for success in life and opening Heaven's vault of abundance.

- *Discipline simply means to train or drill by instruction.*

- *Self-discipline is the bridge between your desires and their fulfillment.*

- *Self-discipline only has one purpose, and that is to form positive habits in our life.*

We are not creatures of discipline but rather, creatures of habit.

# It is through determined **DISCIPLINE** that we give birth to the habits that will ultimately accomplish God's will for our lives.

One of the reasons we may have difficulty creating the right habits is because we attempt to change too many areas of our life at one time. We must be patient with ourselves. I encourage you to take the time to focus on one area of your life that you would like to change, and then begin to apply the necessary discipline to that area.

Forming positive habits requires time and diligence. If we refuse to quit, we see positive habits formed in our lives—habits that bring success.

Successful individuals make a habit of doing the things that failures do not like to do. The things failures don't like to do are the same things successful people don't like to do. But successful people do them anyway because they realize that this is the price they must pay for the success they desire.

# *9 Habits Of Highly <u>Effective</u> Millionaires*

According to a study of college students at the Ernst & Young International Intern Leadership Conference in Orlando, Florida, 59 percent of these young leaders expect to be millionaires within their lifetime. What's more, 5 percent of them expect to hit the million-dollar mark while in their 20s.

And the super-rich is a growing group. The top 0.1 percent of the population's average income was $3 million in 2002, up two and a half times the $1.2 million, adjusted for inflation, that same group reported in 1980.

The typical millionaire isn't what many people picture. But there are some consistent patterns among those people who earn or plan to inherit their money, and these strategies may be worth emulating.

## Habit #1 - Spend Less Than You Earn

*Pay God first! Then pay yourself.*

The best way to accumulate a large amount of money is by taking control of your financial life. God will give you the wisdom and understanding to achieve your financial goal.

The only way to get money to invest is to save regularly. For most people, the only way to save regularly is to spend less than you earn. The only way to spend less than you earn is to change your lifestyle.

After you give 10% (and above) to God, then make it a non-negotiable to save and invest 10% of your income throughout your working life.

Take 10% of your income off the top of your paycheck each time you receive it and put it away into a special account for financial accumulation.

# In order for the seeds of prosperity to grow up within you, you must first be able to <u>SAVE</u> money.

I choose not to live at the maximum affordable lifestyle.

**4 <u>Benefits</u> Of Living Below Your Means:**
1. Ability to give.
2. Flexibility to pursue business opportunities.
3. Maximize retirement investments.
4. Keep connected with friends and family.

## Habit #2 - **Work Hard And Smart**

Being wealthy is a full-time job itself because you have to keep track of where your money is and what it is doing at all times.

Most millionaires don't dump a lot of money into anything without careful consideration and much research.

## 5 _Facts_ About Millionaires And Work

- **All millionaires work extremely hard.** They start their day early, they work very hard during the day, and they stay late. They develop a reputation for being amongst the hardest working people in their field.

- **Millionaires practice the "40 Plus" formula.** This formula says that you work 40 hours per week for survival. Everything over 40 hours is for success. If you only work 40 hours (and the average work week today is closer to 35 hours), all you will ever do is survive. You will never get ahead. You will never be a big financial success. You will never be highly respected and esteemed by your colleagues. You will always be mediocre working the basic 40-hour week. (_Brian Tracy's 21 Millionaire Habits._)

- **Millionaires believe every hour over 40 is an investment in their future.** I can tell where you are going to be in five years by looking at how many productive hours over 40 you put in every week.

- **The typical millionaire works 60 hours per week.** Many of them work 70 and 80 hours.

- **Millionaires work while they work.** They are productive with their time. When they work, they don't waste time. When they get in early, they put their head down and get started immediately.

 **Solomon's List Of The Positive Effects Of Hard Work** *(Proverbs)***:**

- Wealth (10:4, 12:27)
- Wisdom (10:5)
- Abundant supply of food (12:11, 20:13, 28:19)
- Power to lead (12:24)
- Fulfilled desires (13:4)
- Profit (14:23)
- Clarity (15:19)
- Meaningful career (22:29)
- Ample resources (27:23-27)

— Martin Luther (1483-1546)
German reformer and theologian

## "I have held many things in my hands, and I have lost them all. But whatever I have placed in God's hands, that I still possess."

## Solomon's List Of
## <u>Negative</u> Effects Of Laziness *(Proverbs)*:

- Poverty (6:11, 10:4, 14:23, 20:13, 24:33-34, 28:19)
- Family breakdown (10:5)
- Lack of favor (10:26)
- Always following (12:24)
- Distasteful blessings (12:27)
- Uneasiness and lack of contentment (13:4)
- Closed off path (15:19)
- Destruction (18:9)
- Hunger (19:5)
- Always a starter, never a finisher (19:24, 25:15)
- No harvest (20:4)
- Death (21:25)
- Controlled by fear (22:13, 26:13)
- Ruin and decay (24:31)

## Habit #3 - **Know Where Your Money Goes**

Do you know where every single dollar of your monthly income goes? Have you given an assignment to each dollar? Much of it is wasted away here and there, and you may not even really realize how much is spent that way.

## Habit #4 - Eliminate All Debt
*(more about this in Chapter 12)*

The amount of money the average family owes to banks, department stores, and other lending institutions has risen every year for the past thirty years. Consumer debt has increased at an even higher rate than the cost of living. It now represents a much larger percentage of the average worker's earnings.

## Habit #5 - Use Compound Interest To Your Advantage

Compound interest is interest paid on the original amount deposited and on the additional amount accrued. Even if you don't think you can set aside enough money to make it worth it, you can.

# *You Do The Math...*

Compound interest is calculated both on the principal and on all interest accumulated to date. Loans based on compound interest are extremely expensive for the borrower. Avoid them at all cost. But investments yielding compound interest can be very profitable. For example, faithfully investing $500 a year at five percent interest yields $6,289 in a ten-year span, and $16,533 in twenty years. For compound interest to work, you must not withdraw interest as you earn it. The more often interest is paid, the faster your investment grows.

That's enough to send your child to college, help with their first house payment, or to pay for that big wedding. If they let it sit until they are 60, they would be millionaires.

## Habit #6 - Invest In Your 401(k)

There is no reason not to take advantage of your company's 401(k) retirement plan if they offer one. A percentage of your salary is contributed each year, before taxes are taken out, and oftentimes your employer will match a certain percentage of funds as well. Then that money gains interest over time and you have some money saved for retirement, plus, in the present, the amount of taxes you pay is reduced because the money is taken out before taxes. So a 401(k) is doubly wise.

## Habit #7 - Get Yourself Started On An Individual Retirement Account (IRA)

You can have a percentage of your annual income automatically deposited into a separate savings account, and it is not subject to income tax as long as you leave it there. Though it will be taxed once you withdraw it, by the time you do, you probably will be in a lower tax bracket, saving you money. Your IRA fund can be in a bank, or in stocks, bonds, and mutual funds.

## Habit #8 - Open Up A Roth IRA

A Roth IRA is similar to a regular IRA only with more conditions to be met. Your eligibility is based on your income, and is different for singles and married couples. The maximum amount you can contribute starts at $3,000 for the first two years and increases to $5,000 by the sixth year, then $500 a year after that. Contributions to a Roth IRA are not tax deductible; however, earnings and withdrawals are not taxed.

## Habit #9 - Be Generous

During the last half-century, increased wealth has coincided with decreased giving. Pollster George Barna writes, "Generally, the more money a person makes the less likely he is to tithe." Indeed, giving levels were higher during the Great Depression of the 1930s, when incomes were low compared to today.

— John Wesley (1703-91)
English evangelist and
founder of Methodism

## "Earn as much as you can. Save as much as you can. Invest as much as you can. Give as much as you can."

# 20 _Attributes_ Of Wealthy People:

1. LOVE WHAT THEY DO.
2. PERFORM AT THEIR BEST.
3. ADOPT A WILLING ATTITUDE.
4. DO MORE THAN THEY MUST.
5. MANAGE TIME WELL.
6. TAKE INITIATIVE.
7. RADIATE ENTHUSIASM.
8. PERSONIFY DILIGENCE.
9. EXEMPLIFY SELF-DISCIPLINE.
10. PRACTICE ASSERTIVENESS.
11. PART OF A TEAM (OR TEAM PLAYER).
12. RISK DOING SOMETHING GREAT.
13. MAINTAIN CLEAR FOCUS.
14. SET THE STANDARD IN COMPETENCE.
15. ESTABLISH AND PRESERVE ORGANIZATION.
16. RESPECT OTHERS NO MATTER WHAT.
17. COMMUNICATE EFFECTIVELY.
18. DRESS WELL.
19. MODEL CHARACTER.
20. COMMITTED TO CONSTANT CHANGE.

# "One Of The Greatest Laws Of Money Is This... Either Control Money, Or It Will End Up Controlling You."

## – *Robb Thompson*

## Universal Truths Of Increase

**Proverbs 10.16**
The earnings of the godly enhance their lives,
but evil people squander their money on sin.

**Psalm 144.13-15**
May our farms be filled with crops of every kind. May the
flocks in our fields multiply by the thousands, even tens of
thousands, and may our oxen be loaded down with produce.
May there be no breached walls, no forced exile, no cries of
distress in our squares. Yes, happy are those who have it like
this! Happy indeed are those whose God is the Lord.

# Foundational LAWS Of Enduring Wealth

# "The Law Of Abundance Declares, There Is More Than Enough Wealth For Everyone."

*– Robb Thompson*

God is a God of abundance. He really is. God designed this way of living for His children. He came to give us life and life more abundantly. Now, I am not stating that God came to make everyone rich. What I am saying is this: God desires for us to have more than enough finances to take His Gospel to a dying world. I can tell you the answer is not for God to give us more money. We have plenty of money. The issue is how we handle and spend our money.

But remember, first and foremost you must be fully convinced that God is not against abundance. He is against the excess use of it for personal pleasure and gain. He is more interested in what we do with money than He is against the abundance of it.

There is a common misperception that God is somehow displeased with those who earnestly seek their own good. Wherever this erroneous idea originated, it was not from the God of the Bible. Even a cursory glance at a few of the innumerable blessings in Scripture will quickly reveal faith in God's promises to be much more nearly connected to the pursuit of happiness than the most impassioned dreams of a secular hedonist. As author and philosopher C.S. Lewis once said, "When we fool around with drink, sex, and ambition, the problem is not that our Lord finds our desires too strong, but too weak. We are far too easily pleased."

Let's establish this new thought in your mind: There is nothing wrong with you and your family living a good and prosperous life! It is God's portion for you and I. God wants His people to enjoy the abundant life! But that cannot be accomplished unless we are willing to follow the instructions contained in His Word.

The Bible tells us, "Behold that which I have seen: it is good and comely for one to eat and to drink, and to enjoy the good of all of his labor that he taketh under the sun all the days of his life, which God giveth him: for it is his portion" *(Ecclesiastes 5:18).*

And we discover, "Every man also to whom God hath given riches and wealth, and hath given him power to eat thereof, and to take his portion, and to rejoice in his labor; this is the gift of God" *(Ecclesiastes 5:19).*

You may be reading this book not persuaded that God has your best interest in mind. Deep down inside you believe you will always struggle and live paycheck to paycheck. This belief has demobilized you. It is what has kept so many from every truly walking in the abundance that God has prescribed for us in His Word.

There is no lack in the world today. Just look at these striking statistics:

- In 1982, inclusion on the Forbes 400 list of richest Americans required personal wealth of $91 million; at that time, the list included 13 billionaires. By 1998, $500 million was required, and the list included 189 billionaires. In 2007, every member on the list was a billionaire. *(Forbes, The Forbes 400, 2007.)*

- At the turn of the 21st century, the United States was home to 276 billionaires, over 2,500 households with a net worth exceeding $100 million, 350,000 individuals with a net worth of $10 million, and 5 million millionaires. *(Ellen Remmer, What's a Donor to Do? The State of Donor Resources in America Today (Boston: The Philanthropic Initiative, 2000.)*

- In 2007, there were over 400 billionaires in the United States. *(Forbes, The Forbes 400, 2007.)*

- The high-net-worth population (net worth of at least $1 million or $500,000 in investable assets) in North America in 2005 was 2.9 million. This population has more than $10 trillion worth of wealth. *(World Wealth Report: 10th Anniversary Merrill Lynch, 2007; Capgemini, 2006.)*

- Americans (pop. 299.8 million) collectively made $12.4 trillion in income in 2005. *(United Nations Statistics Division, United States-GNI AllSeries.)*

- There are 9,500,000 millionaires in the world, an increase of 11 percent in 2004 alone. *(Capgemini. Merrill Lynch and Capgemini Release 11th Annual World Wealth Report, 2007.)*

There is plenty of wealth in the world today. In fact there is more than enough!

## *Let me put it into perspective for you...*

Let's look at the value of some common substances found on God's earth. During the next twenty years, at today's production rate and values (not counting future inflation), we will produce $51.48 trillion in copper, gold, silver, aluminum, iron, tin, zinc, and lead, and another $52 trillion in oil, barley, corn, meat, rice, and wheat. Add $383 trillion in conservatively estimated world-wide coal reserves and another $600 trillion in non-coal electric energy reserves. These 16 items alone total more than $1,082 trillion in new wealth!

One reliable source estimated that 88 percent, or $134 billion, of all legally circulated U.S. currency is unaccounted for! Federal economists speculate much of it is "on-hand" cash kept in people's pockets or in private stashes under beds, in walls, or buried in backyards. Some is probably overseas, and criminals and drug kingpins – the wicked of our society – have much of it.

Amazingly up to sixty times more $100 bills are in circulation than $1 bills! It is no wonder Christians have so much trouble getting their hands on money. They are going after $1 bills, and those are in shortage! They need to start going after $100 bills!

Remember how a few years ago many said the exploding world population soon would leave no room for anyone? Despite that gloom and doom, the simple truth is: Earth's resources can support our multiplying humanity at higher standards of living than man has every known!

It is said that if we stood all the world's people together without touching – allowing 2.6 square feet for each person – they would fit into the Jacksonville, Florida city limits with plenty of room to spare. Do you honestly think God would allow billions of people on this earth without room enough to live? Of course not. And the earth's ability to absorb man's population is only improving.

## *10 Unbreakable Laws Of Abundance*

### 1. Law Of Priority
**WRONG** *Priorities Sabotage The Man Who is In Search of Prosperity.*
*(Matthew 6:33; Proverbs 3:9-10; Deuteronomy 8:11-18)*

Set priorities on your activities and concentrate single-mindedly on one thing at a time. By continually setting priorities and

concentrating on your highest value tasks, you soon develop the habit of high performance.

When we give to God first, He provides for our needs by adding to what we already have, by blessing our efforts, by providing supernaturally, by sending others to meet our needs, and by preventing decay that would normally wear out our personal possessions. Since financial peace comes only when we seek first His Kingdom, God gave us His guarantee of provision in order to increase our confidence and promote our generosity.

## *The Big Rocks...*

Stephen Covey shares a story in his book, <u>First Things First</u>, which is so true. He said, "I attended a seminar once where the instructor was lecturing on time. At one point, he said, 'Okay, it's time for a quiz.' He reached under the table and pulled out a wide-mouth gallon jar. He set it on the table next to a platter with some fist-sized rocks on it. 'How many of these rocks do you think we can get in the jar?' He asked.

"After we made our guess, he said, 'Okay. Let's find out.' He set one rock in the jar... then another... then another. I don't remember how many he got in, but he got the jar full. Then he asked, 'Is that jar full?'

"Everybody looked at the rocks and said, 'Yes.' Then he said, 'Ahhh.'

"He reached under the table and pulled out a bucket of gravel. Then he dumped some gravel in and shook the jar and the gravel went in all the little spaces left by the big rocks.

"Then he grinned and said once more, 'Is the jar full?' By this time we were on to him. 'Probably not,' we said.

"'Good!' He replied. And he reached under the table and brought out a bucket of sand. He started dumping the sand in and it went in all the little spaces left by the rocks and the gravel. Once more he looked at us and said, 'Is the jar full?'

"'No!' We all roared.

"He said, 'Good!' And he grabbed a pitcher of water and began to pour it in. He got something like a quart of water in that jar. Then he said, 'Well, what's the point?'

"Somebody said, 'Well, there are gaps, and if you really work at it, you can always fit more into your life.'

"'No,' he said, 'that's not the point. The point is this: If you hadn't put these big rocks in first, would you ever have gotten any of them in?'"

## In other words, he was talking about <u>PRIORITIES</u>.

## 2. Law Of Diligence

***The Price Tag Of Prosperity Is Stamped With The Word "<u>DILIGENCE</u>."***
*(Proverbs 10:4-5; 12:24; 13:4; Ephesians 4:28)*

Diligence requires discipline, hard work, and time. In other words, it requires a marked effort.

# For us to delight in the promises of God, we must continually apply <u>DILIGENCE</u> to our efforts.

God's system is not arranged in such a way that a one-time action produces lasting results. God's way of progress requires diligence, faithfulness, and patience. The same principle applies for any endeavor. We cannot expect to be physically fit by exercising one week out of the year. To see positive results, we must continue for several months; and for lasting results, we must make exercise a part of our daily lifestyle! We all want to achieve more and do great things, but we only experience true greatness by diligently applying God's principles to our lives.

Diligence bridges the gap between discipline and reward. Anyone can discipline himself for a day, but only discipline coupled with diligence causes us to lay hold of Heaven's reward.

### 3. Law Of Problem Solving

***The Problems You Solve Determine The <u>REWARDS</u> You Receive.***
*(Joseph - Genesis 41:37-44; David - 1 Samuel 17:25, 45-50;*
*Rahab - Hebrews 11:31; Joshua 2:4-6, 12-16; 6:23)*

It is easy to understand why so many people go unrewarded in life—they rarely seem to understand the correlation between the sacrifices of problem solving that eventually lead to the sure road of promotion. Most people stop progressing upwardly the moment their present environment no longer pleases them.

# The willingness to solve the problems of those we are responsible to in life will quickly reveal the <u>VALUE</u> that we place upon them.

When we begin to passionately solve problems, we receive the favor necessary to bring us the promotion we desire.

Many simply exist at their jobs and in their daily routines, sailing roughly through life's meandering seas, unwilling to serve those around them. We can never grumble about life and expect the blessings of Heaven. Although productivity plays a great role within our lives, our attitude causes our productivity to become pleasing. Everyone loves to be around an individual with a great attitude. Therefore, we must cheerfully and sacrificially solve the problems of those we serve.

**Let us ask:** What problems can we solve for our authorities? What can we do to make their lives more productive?

# The sacrificial fulfillment of these answers brings you ever-increasing promotion. Choose to be a problem solver today!

### 4. Law Of Poverty

*Poverty Is Not The* <u>LACK</u> *Of Money; Poverty Is The Proof Of* <u>MISGUIDED</u> *Money.*
*(Proverbs 11:24-25)*

I remember years ago, when I was a young boy, hearing a conversation between my mother and father. My father inquired of my mother, "What should we buy—beer or bread?" At that time, we didn't have enough money for both, so they had to choose between beer and bread. My mother responded, "Let's buy beer."

It wasn't that my parents didn't have money. They just used their money in the wrong way. God calls us to give a tenth to our church. He calls us to feed the poor and help those less fortunate, and to sow into the lives of others for the good they did in our lives. The moment we begin to follow these instructions is when our days of lack are over.

# When we focus our money in the right direction, money increases.
## We reap only what we sow.

If we don't sow anything, we have no right to expect a harvest. How do you spend your money? Do you see it as a seed, or simply money? Do you generously give it, or do you hoard it? Does it go toward the things of God, or toward fulfilling the lusts of your flesh?

Where your money goes determines whether you walk in abundance or in poverty. Poverty is not the lack of money; poverty is the proof of misguided money. The choice is yours.

 Prosperity is revealed to the heart of a sower; you'll never find it in the life of a hoarder.

### 5. Law Of Association
***A Life Without A Harvest Is Proof You Have Invested In The <u>WRONG</u> People.***
*(Luke 6:38; 2 Chronicles 20:35-37)*

In order for me to walk in abundance, I had to disconnect from past relationships and embrace the relationships of tomorrow.

# The seed can never change the soil; the seed can only reveal the quality of the soil.

**6. Law Of The Seed (Review Chapter 1)**
*Your* **SEEDS** *Of Today Are The Undeveloped Photos In Your Future Scrapbook.*
*(2 Corinthians 9:6-7; Genesis 8:22; Galatians 6:7-9)*

The Scriptures tell us that when we plant a seed, it grows up and produces fruit, even though we don't know how.

God engineered the laws of the universe so that every seed we sow matures and produces a harvest. Some people argue that they have no means to sow, but that simply isn't true. The problem is we look at what we don't have, rather than what we do. Let's begin this moment to look at everything we do have. Because when we resolve to do so, we are always ready to eagerly give.

Now think of how powerful a seed is. Though small at first, it can overturn the concrete in our greatest cities.

# YOUR SEED—your time, heart, money, attitude, words, and skills—can radically transform your life if you let it.

But like Jesus said, you have to be willing to let your seed fall to the ground and "die" so that something can come of it. In fact, you must be willing to make your whole life a seed, dying to yourself so that your life can produce fruit for others. And that's a harvest worth waiting for.

### 7. Law Of The Harvest
*You Will Always* <u>**REAP**</u> *What You Sow.*
*(Galatians 6:7-9)*

Many Christians buckle under pressure and never experience true fulfillment. The enemy attempts to wear us down. If he causes us to grow weary, he limits the size of the harvest we receive. The more we sow, and the longer we are willing to wait for the harvest, the greater the reward. We live in a society that feeds off the desire for instant gratification. Desiring something before we are able to handle it or before our harvest is mature hinders us from walking in abundant life.

I see many young people with high aspirations in life refuse to hold on for the long haul. It is a rarity to find an individual who decides to sow and refuses a harvest today, knowing it will be greater tomorrow.

# We must learn to wait and prepare, knowing that God is <u>**NEVER**</u> late to promote.

## 11 *Principles* Of Harvest

1. **Seed must be planted.**
   *(Ecclesiastes 3:2)*

2. **Seed must be rendered useless.**
   *(John 12:24)*

3. **Seed reproduces after its own kind.**
   *(Genesis 1:12)*

4. **The amount of seed you sow sets your harvest size.**
   *(2 Corinthians 9:6)*

5. **Seed must be planted in good ground.**
   *(Matthew 13:8)*

6. **There is always a wait between seedtime and harvest.**
   *(Mark 4:26-29)*

7. **Crops must be maintained for a proper harvest.**
   *(Matthew 13:7)*

8. **You must always sow to your harvest size, not from it.**
   *(Genesis 26:12)*

9. **Harvest is the most expensive time.**
   (Matthew 20:1)

10. **Part of your harvest is for sowing again.**
    *(2 Corinthians 9:10-11)*

11. **Part of your harvest is for you to keep.**
    *(1 Corinthians 9:7)*

## 8. Law of The Tithe

### *Your Tithe Is The Major Key To Breaking Free From* <u>POVERTY!</u>
*(Malachi 3:6-10)*

- **Personal Tithing:** One out of every 12 adults (8 percent) gave away at least a tithe of their income in 2001. That was marginally above the 6 percent of adults who tithed in 2000. *(George Barna, Americans Were More Generous in 2001 Than in 2000, news release by Barna Research Group, April 9, 2002.)*

- **Household Tithing:** The proportion of U.S. households that tithed their incomes to their churches dropped from 8 percent in 2001 to 3 percent of adults in 2002. *(George Barna, Tithing Down 62% in the Past Year, news release by Barna Research Group, May 19, 2003.)*

- **Percentage Given:** The IRS reports that those who itemize deductions on their income tax returns have claimed, since 1975, that between 1.6 percent and 2.16 percent of their income went to charitable concerns. Gallup polls taken every two years have found charitable donations to run between 1.5 percent and 2 percent of income. *Giving USA,* a definitive report published by American Association of Fund-Raising Counsel, says that giving has ranged between 1.7 percent and 1.95 percent of personal income over the last 20 years. *(Tim Stafford, The Anatomy of a Giver: American Christians Are The Nation's Most Generous Givers, but We Aren't Exactly Sacrificing, Christianity Today, May 19, 1997.)*

# By <u>*Tithing*</u>, *Stewards Demonstrate 4 Things:*

1. They are obedient in financial matters.

2. The wealth they receive is not their own, for it comes from the Master of their stewardship.

3. Heaven will remain open so that their Master will be able to prosper all they do.

4. Faithfulness in tithing stops the devourer from diminishing the harvest of their stewardship.

To receive the optimum God-kind of abundance, you must not overlook or under-emphasize the basic building blocks of your Bible abundance plan. To open Heaven's windows and keep them open, you must tithe. Biblically, tithing is not optional.

You don't want to rob God. He says we rob Him when we don't tithe. We tithe at His command, not our discretion. By faithfully bringing Him the tithe, we establish our honesty and obedience.

In Hebrews 7:1-10 we see that Abraham paid tithes. In fact, Abraham tithed for all posterity – for his natural children (seed), and for the spiritual children (seed) who now live in the dispensation of grace; that means you and me!

The obligation of tithing reaches across the pre-law dispensations, the dispensation of the law, and now into the post-law dispensation of grace. Remember: Faithful tithing opens the windows of heaven, making this basic giving (the tithe) vital.

If the vault of heaven is not open, nothing can flow from God to you or me.

## *4 Facts About The Tithe*

1. The tithe belongs to God.
2. The tithe is always ten percent of your increase
   *(gross and not net).*
3. Tithing is bringing God the firstfruits before paying the bills.
4. The tithe goes into your local church.

**9. Law of Investing**

*Investing Benefits Those Who* <u>**INVESTIGATE**</u> *First.*
*(Luke 14:28-30)*

— Amy Carmichael (1867-1951)
missionary to India

## "You can give without loving.
## But you cannot love without giving."

**Author, Brian Tracy says,**

> # "The only thing easy about money is losing it... Don't lose money... If you think you can afford to lose a little, you're going to end up losing a lot... Only invest with experts who have a proven track record of success in handling money."

## *8 Tips for Successful Investing*

People often want an investment formula. Most financial planners recommend these eight basic principles:

1. **Have a plan** – Even a simple plan can help you take control of your financial future. Review it yearly or if circumstances change.

2. **Start investing as soon as possible** – Make time your ally. Let it put the power of compounding to work for you.

3. **Diversify your portfolio** – By investing in different asset classes – stocks, bonds, and cash – you help protect against poor performance in one investment type while including

investments most likely to help you achieve your important goals.

4. **Invest regularly** – Investing is a process, not a one-time event. By investing regularly over the long term, you reduce the impact of short-term market gyrations. You also attend to your long-term plan before you are tempted to spend those assets on short-term needs.

5. **Maintain a long-term perspective** – For most people, the best discipline is staying invested as market conditions change. Reactive, emotional investment decisions all too often bring regret and principal loss.

6. **Consider growth stocks to help achieve major long-term goals** – Over time, stocks have provided the more powerful returns needed to help your investments' value stay well ahead of inflation.

7. **Keep a comfortable amount of cash in your portfolio** – To meet current needs, including emergencies, use a money market fund or a band account, not your long-term investment assets.

8. **Know what you are buying** – Make sure you understand the potential risks and rewards associated with each of your investments. Ask questions, request information, make up your own mind.

## 10 Guidelines for Choosing a New Investment

It just makes good "cents" to ask the right questions before moving into investments where you have no previous experience or education. Here are ten rules to follow:

1. **Don't invest in anything you don't understand.** – For example, you wouldn't buy a car you didn't know how to drive.

2. **Check out the finances.** – What are the one, five, and ten-year rates of return? What is the debt-to-asset ratio? Find out the investment's track record.

3. **Get it in writing.** – Even if it's your mother's sister's first cousin, demand certain facts in writing. What is the maturity date? Amount returned at maturity? Rate of return? Get everything in writing, even with a fellow "Christian."

4. **Learn from the past.** – Don't make the same mistake twice. Also, check the track record of any investment.

5. **Check out the ratings.** – Is the investment risk rated by Moody's Investors Service, Standard & Poor's, Duff and Phelps, or another well-respected agency? Or is the investment insured by a third party such as FGIC or AMBAC?

6. **Run a credit check.** – Call your state securities division and ask if anyone has filed complaints against the investment seller.

7. **Know what you are paying in fees.** – Even if it appears you pay no commission, the seller gets paid, probably from your annual returns, cash value or management, or maintenance fees. Find out.

8. **Be realistic.** – Risk and return go hand in hand. If it sounds too good to be true, it is. Remember: If you can't afford to lose it, don't invest it.

9. **Never do business over the phone with people you have never met representing companies you have never heard of.**

10. **When in doubt, <u>DON'T</u>!**

— John Calvin (1509-64)
French theologian and reformer

# "If we believe heaven to be our country, it is better for us to transmit our wealth thither, than to retain it here, where we may lose it by a sudden removal."

## 10. Law of Saving
### <u>SAVING</u> *Is Necessary To Wealth Accumulation.*

The ant shows us the wisdom of setting something aside for the future. As a Christian steward, I believe it is wise to have a reasonable cash reserve – an amount you consider prudent in light of your responsibilities.

The foundation stone of your savings plan should always be your dependency upon God to provide. If your family tithes and gives proper offerings, you will place yourself under the open Heaven of God. There, God guarantees to protect you if the unforeseen happens.

Christians should save for the foreseeable future. That might include the major purchases every family must make from time to time, for example: educating your children, special desires such as vacations, and, of course, retirement.

How much should you save? Follow the suggestions outlined in this chapter and I believe you will be safe. Faithfully tithe, give generously into the Kingdom of God, and then set aside enough to cover at least 3-6 months of expenses.

# "If You Are Not Receiving A Financial Harvest, You Must Reevaluate Your Understanding Of God's View Of Prosperity."

## – Robb Thompson

Prosperity Pointer

## Universal Truths Of Increase

### Proverbs 3.9-10

Honor the Lord with your possessions, and with the firstfruits of all your increase; so your barns will be filled with plenty, and your vats will overflow with new wine.

### Luke 6.38

Give, and it will be given to you: good measure, pressed down, shaken together, and running over will be put into your bosom. For with the same measure that you use, it will be measured back to you.

# Lending
# Your MIND
# To What
# You Believe

# "*Your Future Prosperity Lies In The Present Confines Of Your Mind.*"

*– Robb Thompson*

**PROSPERITY** has more to do with your mind than with your pocketbook.

- *Do you believe God wants you to prosper?*
- *Do you believe prosperity is your right as a believer?*
- *Do you believe God wants people to be poor and needy?*

Whatever you believe is evident in your life. Let me explain. People hold many beliefs about life intransigently formed by past experiences and rigidly directed by various people. After years of sustained thought, those viewpoints become beliefs that govern and ultimately control your life.

You and I are stringently governed by the **CORE** **BELIEFS** we hold. We act in accordance to what we truly believe, not just what we say we believe.

If we believe God wants us poor, or that poverty is our destiny, life proves that for us. But if we believe God wants us blessed, life proves this to us as well.

We are a living prophecy of what we believe. What do you believe? Whatever it is, it just might be the very thing that precludes God's blessings from your life. The Israelites believed they were grasshoppers in the sight of the giants and therefore never seized the Promised Land.

# Prosperity is an internal recognition before it is ever an external possession.

Prosperity does not solely consist of one's possessions. God did not design prosperity so we could attain nice cars, expensive jewelry, or fancy homes; He designed it so we would have more than enough to fulfill the assignment given to us. God has nothing against anyone enjoying material things, but we first must seek to fulfill His will before we can ever seek to enjoy the pleasures of this life. Jesus said, "Seek first the Kingdom of God and His righteousness, and all these things shall be added unto you."

Although the world's superstars, the country's top athletes, high paid fashion models, and television's pop artists may have lots of money and toys of a fantasy world, they are far from experiencing true prosperity.

# The prosperity that God desires for His people dwells within the pages of His Word.

As we continue to plant the seed of God's Word into our hearts, we soon see it manifest in our lives. His Word contains the provision we need for every area of our lives.

The Bible tells us that the diligent prosper. Those who diligently receive and fervently act upon the Word of God soon see abundant provision.

I also like to say it like this: **"Prosperity Is Never What Lives In Your Circumstances; Prosperity Is What Bursts Into Life From Within You."**

## 7 Facts About Your Thoughts

Solomon observed, "As a man thinks in his heart, so he is." Another way of saying this is, "As a man thinks within his subconscious, so he will live out to be." Let me go back to the example of the garden and the gardener. James Allen, author of <u>As A Man Thinketh</u>, says, "As the plant springs from, and could not be without, the seed, so every act of a man springs from the hidden seeds of thought, and could not have appeared without them."

Soil will accept flower seeds just as readily as weed seeds. The heart will accept negative destructive thoughts and in time it will produce outer circumstances. It will produce success if positive thoughts are planted in it. This is what is meant by the law of sowing and reaping stated in Galatians 6:7, "Whatever you sow, you will reap."

Your mind is the gardener, and your heart is the garden. Thoughts are seeds which, when planted and watered, produce strongholds or paradigms. These strongholds or paradigms harvest into action and our actions determine our experiences.

Beware, your mind is the dark room where the devil attempts to develop his negatives. But your heart is the soil where planted thoughts (positive or negative) give birth to actions and consequences. English philosopher, John Locke, once observed, "I have always thought the actions of men the best interpreters of their thoughts."

1. Your **HEART** is the Soil Where Your Thoughts Become The Seeds That Create Your Future.
   *(Proverbs 4:23)*

The voices and thoughts that enter your mind are seeds. You have a choice over which seeds get planted and which get rejected. Your heart becomes the fertile soil where those seeds are planted. When planted, those seeds grow up and produce fruit in your life.

There is no way to avoid this process of "heart germination," for the Bible tells us in Proverbs 4:23 that this is how God designed the human heart to function: "Keep [manage, tend, protect, safeguard, watch over, preserve, chaperon, care for, be a good steward over] your heart with all diligence, for out of it spring the issues of life." The only way to assure good outcomes in your life is to plant good seeds in your heart.

**2. Any Thought Left Unchallenged Is Established As <u>FACT</u>.**
   *(2 Corinthians 10:3-5)*

When you don't reject negative beliefs, they begin to dig their claws deeper inside of you. When you don't reject a wrong thought, it begins to develop a hold on you. When you allow negative thinking to remain in your mind, unchallenged, it will soon become your master.

Financial freedom will not come over night. Making the necessary mental changes is a process. Renewing your mind begins the process. It doesn't happen in a day or even in a week. Whatever God does He does step by step, and His work is never destroyed. He knows you wouldn't be able to withstand pressure from change too quickly attained. The spiritual life is continuous growth. Walking in financial freedom is a journey.

**3. If You Never Change Your Thoughts, It Will Be Impossible For You To <u>CHANGE YOUR DESTINY</u>.**
*(Proverbs 23:7)*

Whichever thoughts you plant into the soil of your mind will determine your destiny. Once you've planted God's thoughts concerning abundance and prosperity, be patient. Water your garden and nurture it with by thinking and speaking God's Word. You may not see any sign of growth for a while, but would you dig up a seed to see if it was growing? You trust that it will. You're sure of this because humans have been planting simple seeds for thousands of years with great success.

Western Christianity is challenged by impatience and the desire for instant gratification. We want visual proof that God's Word is growing within us. God's Word will not fail, and it will only produce fruit in God's timing. Truly, you can't know how long it is going to take to create a harvest from the new thought seeds you have sown. Remember, Isaiah 55:11 tells us, "God's Word does not return void."

God instructs us to meditate on the Word, confess the Word, and spend regular, quality time in the Word. That's how we walk in God's will for our life. We have to conquer our carnal minds to experience ultimate financial freedom.

**4. You Will Always Move In The Direction Of Your Most Significant <u>THOUGHTS</u>.**
   *(2 Corinthians 4:18)*

The Law of focus says that whatever you focus on grows. The more you devote yourself to a thought, the more it becomes your reality.

# Prosperous men and women of God <u>DISCIPLINE</u> themselves to think and talk only what God says. They protect their minds from messages that the circumstances of life continually shout at them.

Ralph Waldo Emerson wrote, "A man becomes what he thinks about most of the time." If you want to win the battle of your mind, you must protect the doorways of your mind. Continue to dwell upon what the Scriptures say and refuse to entertain any fear or doubt. You will experience extraordinary progress and achievement, and you'll see what God can do when a child of His commits to focus on His Word.

## 5. The <u>TRANSFORMATION</u> Of One's Life Is Undeniably Linked To The Renewing Of One's Mind.
*(Romans 12:2)*

Changing your life means changing your thinking. Your mind can only hold one thought at a time. Therefore, the easiest way to get rid of negative thoughts is to replace them with positive thoughts. The most effective way to do this is with your spoken words. Your mind has to entertain what your mouth is saying. The mind is never empty; it is always occupied with a thought. Spoken words override unspoken thoughts. By substituting your thoughts, you can replace troubling thoughts with a God-thought that has the power to transform your life.

You can't be filled with fear, doubt, and worry when you constantly meditate upon God's Word. As long as you don't allow negative thoughts to be planted into your mind, you'll discover peace, joy, and happiness. The transformation of your life is linked to your commitment to change the way you think

James Allen says, "Many people are anxious to improve their results, but are unwilling to improve themselves. They therefore remain bound." He is exactly right. Your paradigm must change, and results will follow. Target the cause, not the effect.

Suppose you were watching a movie. You discover the plot is really bad and the acting is terrible. Instead of turning on a different movie, you bash in the TV. Then you bring in a different

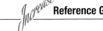

TV and turn on the same movie, hoping this time it will be good!

This is ridiculous of course, but it illustrates a point. The TV plays whatever is placed in the DVD player. The picture on the screen is only the expression of the movie playing in the playback machine. Changing the TV will not make the entertainment any better. The movie itself must be changed.

In life, circumstances, situations, and feelings are only expressions of a movie playing quietly on the inside. Outward changes will eventually find a way to express the internal movie. Only by changing the movie will the outside be permanently changed. If we want to be transformed, we must change the thoughts we allow to dock at our mind. Until we do, the same results will continue to arise.

**6. Your Thoughts Are The <u>COMPASS</u> That Guides The Ship Of Life Into Your Port Of Desire.**

Whatever you allow to harbor in your mind and dwell upon in your thoughts are seeds that develop and produce after their own kind. All thoughts that suggest weakness, failure, unhappiness, or poverty are harmful and self-destructive.

- ***We must see those thoughts as enemies attempting to break out into manifestation.***

- ***We must counterattack those thoughts whenever they try to gain ascendancy in our minds.***

- **We must avoid them as we would thieves...for they truly are...and of the highest degree.**

Our minds must be kept free from devastating bitterness, resentment, hatred, suspicion, and everything that does not line up with God's thoughts. The apostle Paul tells us, "I see another law in my members, warring against the laws of my mind, and bringing me into captivity to the law of sin which is in my members."

We are in a battle, and we must choose to get on the battleship called "Godly Thinking" if we are ever going to experience Heaven's best. God gave us the weapons with which to fight. We are to pull down and bring every negative thought into the obedience of Christ. If He did not say it, then we should not think it.

## 7. Your Life Today Is The Result Of Your <u>THOUGHTS</u> Of Yesterday.

The life you experience tomorrow is the direct result of the thoughts you plant today. When nagging, distracting, negative voices begin to torment your mind, you have to make the wise choice by saying:

- **No, I'm not listening to that!**
- **I'm going to believe the Word, no matter what.**
- **I'm not going to give up; I'm not going to yank God's Word out of my heart.**
- **God's Word is everything to me.**

No matter what you hear or from whom you hear it, search and discover what God has to say about it.

Don't care what anybody else says; find out what God says, and that's what you should believe! That's what you should plant securely inside your heart!

## *4 Laws Of The Mind:*

### 1. Law Of Belief
*Whatever You Believe With Strong Conviction Becomes Your Reality.*

### 2. Law Of Expectation
*Whatever You Expect With Confidence Becomes Your Own Self-fulfilling Prophecy.*

### 3. Law Of Correspondence
*Your Outer World Is A Reflection Of Your Inner World.*

### 4. Law Of Substitution
*Your Mind Can Only Hold One Thought At A Time, And You Can Substitute One Thought With Another.*

## 2 Simple <u>Analogies</u> To Help Understand Mind Prosperity:

### 1. The Jungle

The process of renewing your mind is like cutting a new path through a dense jungle. Your established paradigms are well-traveled paths. These paths are easy to walk on, but they will lead you to the same destination. Reaching a new destination requires a lot of work, discomfort, and bruises. There's a medical center at your new destination, but you'll only be able to recuperate once you've made your new path as clear as your previous ones.

Studies now say, approximately 65% of your unconscious thoughts are the same day to day, and estimate that 95% of these thoughts err to the negative side. These are thoughts you don't even realize you're thinking. These thoughts are well-worn paths in the jungle of your mind. It is easy to continue in these thought patterns because they are the paths of least resistance.

Many psychologists estimate it take 3 to 5 weeks to create a new thought pattern. This is important to understand because when the apostle Paul tells us to "change the way we think in order to transform our lives," he doesn't tell us how long it will take. The timeframe depends on your diligence in cutting or creating a new path. For some it may take just 3 weeks to alter their thought pattern in a certain area of their life. For others, it could take years. It is dependent upon one's desire and commitment to change.

With discipline, perseverance, and new habits, your new pathway will become easier to travel than your old one. If you will travel only on your new path, the old one will eventually be swallowed by your new way of thinking. Your old paradigm will be gone, and the new paradigm will be the easiest and most comfortable path to travel.

## 2. Mental Prisons

Our paradigm is the sum total of our beliefs, values, identity, expectations, attitude, and thought pattern–about us and the world around us. Your paradigm is shaped by past experiences, present expectations, and future hopes. It is the filter through which we view life. We react to life based upon our own paradigm. A paradigm is a person telling himself, "I will always be poor. God doesn't want to bless me. I'll never achieve financial freedom." Another person may have the paradigm, "I am destined to win. God is on my side. If He is for me, who can be against me?" Paradigms are the magnets that attract to us what we believe about life.

What you hear through the media, entertainment, and your circle of influence constantly reinforces or restructures your paradigm. Their messages are usually detrimental to God's image of you.

Why is it that modern Western Christians have every convenience and comfort imaginable, but they are among some of the most unhappy people I have ever met? It would seem that we should be truly content—we have both the promise of eternal life and the ability to prosper in this life. Something is wrong. Though we have accepted Christ as our Savior, we have yet to walk in the abundant life He came to give us.

W. Clement Stone, author of <u>Success Through A Positive Mental Attitude</u>, said, "You are a product of your environment. So choose the environment that will best develop you toward your objective. Analyze your life in terms of your environment. Are the things around you helping you toward success—or are they holding you back?" He confirms what Jesus told us, "According to your beliefs (paradigms) it shall be done unto you" *(Matthew 8:13)*.

Almost 95% of your beliefs are programmed into your internal hard drive by the age of 13. Many of us have been programmed for the negative. We have accepted thoughts such as, "You can't do that," "You'll never succeed," "You're unworthy," "God doesn't love you," "There's nothing special about you," "You'll always be broke," "No one cares about you," "It's just you against the world," "You'll never be financially free," "All rich people are crooks," and the list can go on and on.

These paradigms are prisons. They cannot be seen or felt, and receiving salvation doesn't dissolve them. You must be serious about change. You must be willing to plant the seeds of God's

Word if you want to see a harvest of Christ's character in your life. If what you see is not what you want, then you must plant new seed.

Look at what the enemy is doing. Grab a newspaper, watch the evening news, or listen to the latest music hits. How many messages can you find that communicate fear, poverty, worry, anxiety, illness, failure, or death? What you continue to think about gets planted into your mind.

How can you change the paradigms that keep you from the victory and abundance God has given to you? To get rid of old, negative beliefs, we have to consistently plant new thoughts into our minds. New thoughts, when communicated more strongly than subconscious thoughts, create new paradigms. Joel Arthur Barker writes in <u>Paradigms</u>, "To ignore the power of paradigms to influence your judgment is to put yourself at risk when exploring the future. To be able to shape your future, you have to be ready and able to change your paradigm."

## *6 <u>Mindsets</u> That Oppose Poverty*

1. **It is God's desire that I prosper.** *(3 John 2)*
2. **God thinks nothing is too good for me.** *(Proverbs 24:4)*
3. **God wants me to have the best.** *(Psalm 35:27)*
4. **I am an obedient giver.** *(Malachi 3:8)*
5. **God gives me the power to get wealth.** *(Deuteronomy 8:18)*
6. **This world's wealth can and will come into my hands.**
   *(Proverbs 13:22)*

# 6 Effective <u>Strategies</u> To Renew Your Mind

**1. Clarify:** Identify the beliefs you desire to change.

**2. Leverage:** Write down every negative result of continuing with those beliefs.

**3. Replace:** Develop an alternate belief about the issue at hand. *Here is a template: "Never again will I believe _____ (negative thought) because God has said, _____ (positive thought)."*

**4. Reinforce:** Verbally speak God's Word throughout the day.

**5. Filter:** Filter your thoughts through the Law of Philippians 4:8. Below are criteria for acceptable thoughts. If a thought does not fit into these categories, then it must be replaced. Thoughts must be:
- **True**
- **Noble**
- **Just**
- **Pure**
- **Good**
- **Virtuous**
- **Excellent**

**6. Persist:** Consistently meditate on God's thoughts. *Meditation, while often associated with Eastern mysticism, is simply the practice of going over and over a thought until an internal picture is well formed.*

As the picture becomes clear, it leads to changes in a paradigm and eventually changes in circumstances.

— C.S. Lewis (1898-1963)
English author and scholar

"I do not believe one can settle how much we ought to give. I am afraid the only safe rule is to give more than we can spare. In other words, if our expenditure on comforts, luxuries, amusements, etc., is up to the standard common among those with the same income as our own, we are probably giving away too little...if our charities do not at all pinch or hamper us, I should say they are too small. There ought to be things we should like to do and cannot do because our charitable expenditures excludes them."

**"The Skill Of Managing Your Mind Is One Of The Most Important Skills Along The Journey To Success And Happiness."**

– *Robb Thompson*

# "All Of Us Have Twenty-four Hours Each Day. The Only Difference Between Any Of Us Is How We Spend Them."

## – Robb Thompson

## Universal Truths Of Increase

**Psalm 75.10**
For God says, "I will cut off the strength of the wicked, but I will increase the power of the godly."

**Psalm 107.38**
How He blesses them! They raise large families there, and their herds of cattle increase.

# INVESTING
# Time More
# Effectively

# *"Lack Of Time Can't Produce Failure; Only Mismanaged Time Can."*

*— Robb Thompson*

The excuse of not having enough time is a safe haven for many individuals who want to justify their lack of productivity. But let's be entirely honest with ourselves. Most people have poor time management skills, which, in turn, lend to poor circumstances.

## *5 Crucial <u>Questions</u> When It Comes Time Management:*

1. *How much of your time goes to waste on a daily basis?*

2. *Do you often have five, ten, or fifteen minutes without a clear focus?*

3. *Do you spend time lingering in thoughts and actions that are unnecessary and unfruitful?*

4. *Do you keep track of your time?*

5. *Do you know what you need to accomplish each day?*

Planning your hours is a difficult task initially, but once you get the hang of it, you'll see how much time you actually have! You can be successful, not just financially, but in every area of your life. One of the requirements, though, is that you **LEARN TO MAKE EVERY MOMENT OF YOUR DAY WORTHWHILE.**

I'm sure you have a lot to accomplish, so make it happen, and refuse to make excuses. Doing so always leads you closer to your dreams than ever before.

Go after what you want, but realize this: You can't do everything. You only have twenty-four hours in a day. Every minute takes you either closer to or farther from your intended destiny.

Therefore, you need to ask yourself:

## "WHAT'S THE MOST <u>VALUABLE</u> USE OF MY TIME?"

Your top priority should be to accomplish the purpose for which you were born. Everything in your life must revolve around this goal.

I have learned that I can no longer just *do what I want to do*—instead, *I do what I **must** do.* Only those who want to live in mediocrity "do what they want." Unless you can manage your time and use it to invest into your future, you will not succeed.

# **IF** you do not use the twenty-four hours you have to invest into yourself, you will not attain the prosperity you rightfully deserve.

Identify and eliminate any habit, relationship, interest, or activity that hinders you from pursuing your life assignment. If you are going to *multiply* what has been invested into you, you can't hold on to anything that subtracts or divides! What eats up your time? What hinders you from moving towards success? What books can you read to show you how to succeed? Benjamin Franklin said it like this, **"Waste your time and waste your life for that is what life is made of."** Let me remind you,

All of us have twenty-four hours each day. The only difference between any of us is how we spend them.

The most common form of stress people experience is anxiety from too much to do and too little time in which to do it. In fact, time issues are the greatest struggle in people's lives today. There is simply not enough time to do everything that needs to be accomplished.

The solution to this problem is the ability to master your time. You aren't going to get more than 24 hours; tasks won't decrease, and time won't stop. Therefore, learning to manage your time is the only option. Regardless if you feel you know how to manage your time effectively, there is always room to grow.

# 11 _Keys_ To Master Your Time:

1. **The Investment Of Time Is The First Prerequisite To Performing Your Duties In Excellence.**

Don't waste time by doing something half-heartedly. Give it everything you have. Make the final product a memory of your best rather than a reminder of corners cut. Time once used is gone forever. The only way to live without regret is to do your best with what you have. Give your best effort and you will never be disappointed.

2. **Value Time As You Would Value Money.**

If you do not respect your time, you will not enjoy your future. No great future is promised to those who disrespect their time in the present. Cherish time and you will be richly rewarded.

3. **Document Your Time On A Weekly Basis.**

Do you know where your time goes? Make up a time log, and keep an accurate daily record for one month. You'll be amazed at the amount of time you use unwisely.

This is the same application finance consultants use to teach people to manage their money. When people don't know where their money goes, they believe they don't have enough of it. When people don't know where their time goes, they think the same thing.

### 4. Budget Your Time; Allot It Only In Necessary Segments.

Once you understand where your time goes, you must learn how to budget it to get the most out of it. You have 168 hours per week. How you spend those hours is your choice. Budgeting your time begins with a plan. Plan your day and then diligently work your plan. Take time every morning to plan out your day. Five minutes spent planning may save you hours by the end of the day.

### 5. Make It Known – "My Time Must Be Respected."

This is the key to fighting off those time vampires, the individuals who waste your time with endless conversation and pointless interruptions. Everyone should not have the same access into your life. Others should have to earn or qualify for your time. You cannot simply visit the President of the United States because you want to. You must qualify for his time. Why should it be any different for your time? It shouldn't.

## Don't allow others to waste your time. Make it known that your time must be <u>RESPECTED</u>.

**6. Invest Time With Experts Of Your Chosen Field.**

You must do whatever is necessary to get time with those older than you. Find a way to pursue the knowledge and expertise of those who hold the position you want. Posture yourself as a student and sit at their feet ready to listen. They will teach you what to do and what not to do. Learn from their mistakes and determine not to make the same ones.

**7. Invest Time Within Your Day To Grow As An Individual.**

You need time to be alone. It is not selfish to look after yourself. You cannot help anyone when you are not taken care of. The time you take to develop your character and hone your skills will open doors of opportunity for you.

**8. Take Time To Plan Your Day.**

Planning your day ahead of time increases your productivity by nearly 25%. Remember, those who fail to plan, plan to fail. Become part of the small percentage that refuses to live out their day before it is on paper. My good friend, Dr. Mike Murdock, says,

# "The **SECRET** of your future is hidden within your daily habits."

### 9. Have A Clear Vision For Life.

I believe the first step in time management is a vision for your life. Let me explain it like this: Time is like a closet. Every hour is a shelf that needs to be filled. When arranging your closet, you must keep in mind how you want items to look. How do you want your closet to look in the end? The picture you have influences where you put your belongings.

# The same holds true with your time. A <u>PICTURE</u> of where you want to be in the coming future influences where your time goes.

### 10. Establish Time Constraints In Everything You Do.

Have a deadline for everything you do. To help keep track of your time with larger tasks, set up small goals to measure your progress. Putting time limits on your life may seem like an inconvenience at first, but you'll see the results in your work.

### 11. Stop Allowing Time To Slip Through Your Fingers.

How can you steal your own time? By not planning it! Your time is your life, and it shouldn't be wasted.

# 10 Tips To Help <u>Plan</u> Your Day

1. **<u>IMAGINE</u> your long-term picture of success and put it in writing.** Review your goal often. Your goal should be specific, measurable, achievable, and compatible with where you are now.

2. **Try to do your planning at the <u>SAME</u> <u>TIME</u> every day.** Use this time to review past accomplishments as well as future things to do.

3. **<u>WRITE</u> out an "Action Items" list every day.** You do this by asking the question, "What needs to get done?"

4. **<u>PRIORITIZE</u> your "Action Items" list into A, B, and C priorities.** "A" items are important to your long-term success, "B" may be urgent but not as important, and "C" are those that would be nice to do if you get the time.

5. **Always work on your "A" items until <u>COMPLETED</u>.** Don't work on a "C" just because it's easy to do.

6. **<u>MARK</u> <u>OFF</u> items when completed.** This will give you a sense of accomplishment.

7. **<u>BE</u> <u>CAREFUL</u> not to bottleneck your day full of activities.** Leave time for urgent issues that may come up.

8. **<u>DO</u> <u>IT</u> <u>NOW!</u> Don't procrastinate what is important.** And don't spend all your time on what is urgent.

9. **Always plan time for <u>BALANCE</u>; include family, fitness, recreation, and social and spiritual activities.**

10. **<u>EVALUATE</u> your time and determine your most productive hours; fill that time with your important tasks.** When do you work best? Utilize that time!

The area in which you invest your time determines how you live your life.

## *5 <u>Steps</u> to Simplifying Your Daily Life:*

1. **Get rid of all unnecessary clutter in your life.**

2. **Take a break every 90-120 min.** Set aside time to be with God and in His Word. Exercise. Eat something.

3. **Go through your car, closet, and home and get rid of everything you don't need.**

4. **Take a break from watching television.** Set up a time restriction to your television viewing. Replace it with reading

5. **<u>Implement</u> the time mastery principles above.**

**"The Meaning Of Financial Freedom Is Elusive Until You Unlock The Hidden Treasure Found Within The Pages Of God's Word."**

*– Robb Thompson*

# "Habits Will Determine Our Ultimate Success Or Eventual Failure In Life."

### – Robb Thompson

## Universal Truths Of Increase

### Deuteronomy 1.11
May the Lord make you increase,
both you and your children.

### Psalm 132.17
Here I will increase the power of David;
My anointed one will be a light for My people.

# EXCELLENT
# Returns VS.
# Mediocre
# Yields

# *"Today's Excellence Is Tomorrow's Mediocrity."*

*— Robb Thompson*

Life was designed to be a continual ascension. Excellence is, by its very definition, *progressive*. You cannot expect your level of excellence today to continue over into tomorrow. In order to excel, we must be willing to change for the better.

In our contemporary culture, there is a magnetic pull towards mediocrity. People foolishly attempt to get by in life with the attitude of "just good enough." That mentality eventually debilitates a person's potential.

## The moment we do not press forward, we move backward. We must continually rise above the temptation to accept the **STATUS QUO**.

The individual who does not desire to excel is deceived into thinking that going further is not worth the effort. However,

God wants more for us. The desire to excel is really the desire for a fuller, richer, and more abundant life, which stems from God. When God enters a life, He deposits a relentless desire for betterment.

Many quickly reject that desire, either because they have been taught conversely or because they consciously choose laziness. Nevertheless, we must give our attention to principles of excellence.

So, no matter what level you are today, tomorrow you should be ready to move up to a higher one. You have been designed for movement and change!

## *The Excellent Vs. The Mediocre:*

**The Excellent....**

- Stay one step ahead of the ordinary.

- Do a common thing in an uncommon way.

- Go beyond the status quo.

- Are not satisfied with "just-good-enough" — they know that in real life, it really never is!

- Do their absolute best in every circumstance.

- Understand that today's excellence is tomorrow's mediocrity.

**The Mediocre...**

- Deliver a second-class performance or product.

- Are happy with "just-good-enough."

- Are frail and inadequate.

- Are substandard and inferior.

- Are commonplace and ordinary.

Here is a great rule for success:

# "Your life only gets better when you get better." And since there is no limit to how much better you can become, there is no limit to how much better you can make your life.

## *5 Pillars Of Excellence:*

**Pillar #1** - **The Biggest Difference Between Excellence And Mediocrity Is <u>Finishing</u>.**

People talk about pursuing excellence all the time, but truly there are only a handful of individuals who accomplish it. I am not interested in just talking about or hearing about excellence

— I want to do it and see it expressed in those around me. I'm determined to keep on pressing forward!

That's the stance you must take in order to be a person of excellence. You can't expect to live your life from a place of comfort and still achieve success. Be okay with stretching yourself beyond your comfort zone — continue to go above and beyond in every area of your life, whether it's your personal accomplishments, your giving, or your role in the workplace.

To see the rewards of life come your way, you can't just talk about your goals. Your goals must turn into *action*. Most people never get to the point where they turn their words into actions. They deceive themselves by *saying* they have great dreams and goals without ever *doing* anything to make those dreams come true.

We can't just sit around and *think* about what we want to accomplish with our lives. Get honest with yourself, and take *action*.

**Pillar #2 - Excellence Is A <u>Journey</u>, Not A Destination; It Is A <u>Process</u>, Not An Event.**

There are all kinds of lists in the world: best seller, government watch, crime statistical, animal endangerment, trendy dress, and weekly shopping lists. But excellence is not simply another list, filled with principles to be checked off as though on our daily "to-do" list. Nor is excellence reaching a particular destination.

Excellence is a journey. It is becoming the very person God destined you to become.

Heaven's message is clear:

## A casual attitude towards life leads us to a place of disappointment and defeat.

If we want to realize God's best and go further than our present state, we must answer His call, launching out on the jet that leads us to a lifelong mission of excellence. Too often people say they want excellence in their lives, but they stop pursuing excellence because the price is too high. Many people become discouraged and quit the moment they realize excellence requires a daily striving for improvement. They are simply unwilling to pay the price to obtain the prize.

## <u>EXCELLENCE</u> is something we must pursue continually, something we must earnestly seek, like water in a dry, barren land. It is the quest to become healthy in all areas of life.

We must ask ourselves, "Why should I embrace this message of excellence?" Because the existence of God living within you demands that you improve—daily.

**Pillar #3 - Excellence Is The Passionate Pursuit Of <u>Distinction</u>.**

Have you ever wondered why you possess the apt ability to tally the tip at a restaurant in five seconds flat, while tipping a palm-sized golf ball into a grassy hole seems an utter impossibility? In what very distinctive ways has God set you apart from those around you? No two people are fashioned exactly alike by our artistic Creator. You are unique – an exceptional handiwork of esteemed value. God put something extraordinary on the inside of you that no one else has; He gave you an assignment that belongs exclusively to you. What is it, you may eagerly ask.

# Genuine distinction comes only to those who work hard to achieve it.

**Distinction** – mind, body, and spirit – isn't painless, as portrayed by some; but neither is it the cruel taskmaster that others often perceive it to be. Of course, true distinction won't indiscriminately show up in your life simply because you don a polite smile or wish for it to grace your front door.

Well-known author, James Allen, said, *"Achievement is the crown of effort."* Far too few of us accept the fact that achievement never comes without a significant sacrifice.

# The rewards of life are only distributed to those who choose to embrace the art of distinction.

How do you define distinction in today's confusing world? Distinction isn't just money or fame or success. It is living a life of fulfillment, knowing you are achieving the purpose for which you exist. By learning His ways, His distinction will be made clear inside your life *(check out my book Art of Distinction).*

**PILLAR #4 - All Men Want To Excel, But Few Are Willing To Pay The Price.**

Sacrifice—this principle stands true in any area of life—diets, stronger relationship with God, finances, intimacy between spouses, etc.

Or perhaps I can state it this way: Life gives us what we work for, not what we think we should have. The Bible says, "Go to the ant you sluggard! Consider her way and be wise, which, having no captain, overseer or ruler, provides her supplies in the summer, and gathers her food in the harvest."

Excellence doesn't just happen by chance. You have to passionately and diligently pursue it. Excellence comes with a price tag, but I guarantee it is cheaper than compromise. Compromise costs your life, whereas excellence asks you to give 100% every day. Make every day count. Live as though today was your last day on earth. Learn sacrifice, and obtain the prize by:

- *Paying any price to change.*

- *Paying the price to have a deeper relationship with God.*

You'll never be the same once you make the dedicated decision to pursue excellence in every area of your life.

**Pillar #5 - When There Is More Than One Path To Follow, Always <u>Choose</u> The Excellent.**

The high road is the road God desires for us to take in every situation we encounter. We may think that the devil is our greatest enemy, but the truth is, mediocrity – settling for something less than God's best – is a greater enemy. That is why we have to determine that we will always pursue the divine in every area of our lives.

One of the problems I have discovered in the body of Christ today is that so many individuals live in mediocrity; yet God called us to take the people for whom we are responsible to a higher level. We must be the ones to take a stand and show others how to live a life full of God.

We have been given a divine mandate to help people eliminate the "just good enough" attitude – the attitude that says, "What I do with my life is good enough. Everything is just fine; I don't need to change." We must continue to press for a better life every day.

> # The excellence we live today is not good enough for tomorrow.

Jesus gave His excellence in everything He did—therefore, we, in turn, must desire to give Jesus more tomorrow than what we gave Him today.

### *Let me give you a quick profile of a mediocre individual:*

 If you see yourself at all as you go through this checklist, I encourage you to shake off that "just-good-enough" attitude and focus on turning your intentions into completions.

- "Kills" time by sitting around visiting or doing nothing.

- Continually watches the clock, anticipating the next break or the end of the day.

- Regularly looks for ways to delay work or avoid it altogether.

- Is irresponsible, and then expects others to pick up the slack.

- Acts "put out" and irritated when asked to increase efficiency or workload.

- Becomes an expert at looking busy, yet accomplishes nothing.

- Moves to a new project before completing the last one.

- Blames others for incomplete work.

- Is unwilling to pay the price to get to the next level.

- Puts more thought into vacations than into the future.

- Has many dreams and desires, but never sees them fulfilled.

— Anne Swetchine (1782-1857)
Russian-French writer

# "We are rich only through what we give: and poor only through what we refuse and keep."

# "No One On Earth Can Stop The Advancement Of A True Problem Solver."

*– Robb Thompson*

## Universal Truths Of Increase

### Job 1.10
May there be abundant crops throughout the land, flourishing even on the mountaintops. May the fruit trees flourish as they do in Lebanon, sprouting up like grass in a field.

### Deuteronomy 6.3
You have always protected him and his home and his property from harm. You have made him prosperous in everything he does. Look how rich he is!

# Maximum
# Rules Of
# PROBLEM
# SOLVING

# "Problem Solving Is Doing More Than You Need To Before You're Ever Asked To — Not Because You Have To, But Because You Want To."

*— Robb Thompson*

No matter what kinds of circumstances we face, we were created to win. We have been equipped with the tools necessary to turn any losing situation into an ultimate triumph. Yet in spite of it all, many lose in the game of life. I have always been very interested in knowing why this is the case.

How do doors of opportunity and promotion open for us in life, so we can use our gifts and abilities to their fullest extent?

**Everything Created Solves A Problem.**

Do you realize that every single thing on earth was created to solve a problem? Living organisms solve food chain problems, new inventions solve man-made problems, and so forth.

In the workplace, different occupations solve different problems.

- **Doctors solve health problems.**
- **Dentists solve dental problems.**
- **Lawyers solve legal problems.**
- **Ministers solve spiritual problems.**
- **Teachers solve intellectual problems.**
- **Chefs solve appetite problems.**

Every problem in life has a solution. And *you* have been designed *to be the answer to somebody's problem!* You have a valuable contribution to make; someone needs the answers that only you can provide. The key to your future lies in finding those people and solving those problems!

What problems are you here to solve? Choose, on purpose, to solve problems. You will create a successful outcome for your life, no matter how bad things look for you today.

One of the greatest lessons I have learned in the arena of success is this:

# The most valuable person you will ever encounter in life is a <u>GENUINE</u> problem solver.

Daniel was known as a man who could solve difficult problems. His devotion to excellence and growth was unprecedented, and those traits brought him before greatness. His rewards were no laughing matter—high positions of governmental authority in one of the greatest empires of all time, an array of lavish riches, fine clothing, and honor. At times, Daniel was the sole individual who could solve the problem at hand. That made him the most valuable person around.

So, how about you?

- *Can the same be said of you, that you have a daily commitment to excellence and growth?*

- *Do you prepare to solve greater problems?*

- *Do you make yourself available for those who can bring promotion to your life?*

As we've seen with Daniel, there is a hefty price to pay for these noble ideals, but as we've also seen, the **REWARD** is well worth it.

May God help you to recognize and solve the problems that will bring the greatest return to your life!

# 5 _Keys_ To Unlock The "Problem Solver" Within You.

1. **Finances Are The Reward Of The One Who Makes Problem Solving His Focus.**

Prosperity is simply the reward for solving problems. This is one of the major reasons millions of people attend financial seminars and hear wealth-building principles week after week and still remain poor. They never learned the art of problem solving.

When business leaders and financial advisors teach about wealth, they need to teach about problem solving, because that is the means by which all wealth comes.

# Money is rewarded to those who choose to solve problems.

Once you become a problem solver, opportunity for advancement is easy. There is rarely any competition in problem solving.

Everyone will think you're a fool because you constantly look for ways to serve and help the people around you. But in the end, they will see that the rewards for a problem solver are promotion and prosperity!

## 2. Value In Life Does Not Come From Race, Color, Or Creed, But By The Problems You're Willing To Solve For Others.

Do you realize that by 1995 the most dynamic and rapidly growing economies in the world were right there on the Asian Continent, particularly the nations along the Pacific Rim? By practicing free enterprise, capitalism, and encouraging small businesses, backed by their legendary lifestyle of discipline, nations like Taiwan, South Korea, and Singapore grew to solve problems for people all over the world.

This principle can become easily misinterpreted if you don't understand it—I don't choose to become what other people need because I'm afraid of what may happen if I don't. In other words, I do not passively allow myself to be molded by another person.

# I **BECOME** what is necessary to others, because I realize that doing so gives me a real reason to be in relationship with that person.

I am in relationship to add value, not just to hang around. Similar to the way in which the Asian nations have filled in the gap, I add value the moment I begin to solve problems for other

people. I am the one they seek, because I possess concrete answers and specific solutions to their problems.

Many people grow very frustrated in life because they don't see a purpose in what they do. They feel valueless and unappreciated. Do you know the cure for this? Become what another needs. Answer questions no one else can answer. Keep promises others break. Be willing to go where no one else will go. Be willing to do what no one else will do, and do it well. Take a moment and think about the relationships you are currently in—*How do you add value to their life? What problems do you solve? What answers do you bring?*

3. **A Problem Solver Is Irreplaceable, Choosing To Solve The Problems Others Refuse To Face.**

- ***What problems do you solve?***

- ***Are you called upon to solve the problems at which others sneer?***

- ***Are you willing to do whatever is asked of you?***

After addressing the top 250 business leaders and top executives of a certain nation on this subject, my host, the First Lady of the country, leaned over to me and said, "If my people could embrace what you just taught us, I am confident that our economic problems would dissipate."

### 4. No One On Earth Can Stop The Advancement Of A Problem Solver.

You have to get that fact planted deep in your heart. *No one can stop you!* People may want to set up roadblocks to keep you from moving upward, but you'll just sidestep those roadblocks and keep on rising to the next level!

Your social or economic status doesn't really matter — it does not matter whether you are at the top of the ladder or on the bottom rung. You *will* receive back the good things you do for others! As you solve problems for others, your prosperity and promotion will come.

It doesn't matter if people try to stand in your way. It doesn't matter if your employer disappoints you, puts you down, or even throws you out. All you need to do is maintain your commitment to integrity and continue to be a problem solver for others.

*Then, whatever you make happen for others, the same will happen for you!*

### 5. To Receive Greater Rewards, All One Must Do Is Solve Greater Problems.

The person who cleans the bathrooms may very well be a wonderful person, and I am deeply grateful for such people! Where would we be without them? But as long as cleaning bathrooms is

the problem this person chooses to solve with his life, his choice determines that he will live within the means of a limited amount of finances. He won't go far beyond that level of wages until he begins to solve a higher level of problems for someone else.

One person may hold a secretarial job and earn $8.00 an hour. Another person is an attorney, and his clients pay him $300.00 an hour. Why is this? The reason is not that the secretary has less value as a person than the attorney. It is just that the attorney solves a greater problem. The type of problems a person solves for others determines the amount he is recompensed for his labor.

## *7 Ways To Be A More Attentive Problem Solver* (Excerpt from my book, Passport To Promotion)

**1. Don't just hear – listen.**
Discover what would be considered a job well done. Listen, so you can give your superior what he really wants.

**2. Write it down.**
When you write down your instructions, you show that you value what is being said, and that you will do what you are told. Don't trust your memory. It is estimated that the short-term memory will only store something for forty seconds. Always have a paper and a pen ready. Your boss will be more detailed when he sees

you writing; and the more detailed his instructions, the more excellence you can apply to fulfilling his request.

### 3. Interpret it back to your superior.

Always repeat back what you thought you heard the speaker say. You may have heard something other than what was meant. When you reiterate what was said, your boss will know you understand, or he'll correct your misunderstandings. This step will save you time in the long run.

### 4. Ask them to prioritize their instructions.

When given a list of things to do, ask which items are most important. Complete them in order of importance. What you think is important may not be as important to your employer.

### 5. Act quickly.

Get to work immediately, remembering that accuracy is more important than speed. Combine both as much as possible.

### 6. Report back.

Keep your boss up to date on your progress. Lack of communication breeds uncertainty. You should never have to be asked for a progress report. Make it your responsibility.

### 7. Never complain.

You may say, "I never say anything negative to my boss or my fellow employees." I commend you on that, but complaining

doesn't always have to be voiced. It can be communicated by body language. How do you respond when your boss gives you an instruction? Do you smile and welcome it, or do you show that you are not happy to hear what he has to say? Your body language makes a big difference.

## 3 _Ways_ You Can Be Happy On Your Job

**1.  Decide for whom you work.** "Whatever may be your task, work at it heartily (from the soul), as (something done) for the Lord and not for men" *(Colossians 3:23 AMP)*. It's time to give your job to God.

**2.  Ask God what attitude He wants you to have about your job.** Ask Him what you can do to develop a positive attitude. Remember, God is more interested in your character than in your career status.

**3.  Implement the following seven ways you can increase your job effectiveness and contribute more to your company.** Be specific. Set a timetable for accomplishing each task. Don't wait for your job to become more interesting. Take the initiative and produce more during work. Always remember, activity and productivity are different.

# *7 Hints To Help You Be A More Effective Problem Solver*

(a) **Start work earlier and leave later.** Don't brag about your long hours. Let God give you favor so your extra effort is noticed. Become goal oriented, not clock oriented.

(b) **Be enthusiastic, whatever your work.** Enthusiasm is contagious! If you are excited about your product or service, your customer will be, too.

(c) **Plan your calendar for a month.** List the specific duties you want to achieve on the job and the date by which you plan to attain those goals. If you sell, plan ways to increase your sales calls by at least twenty-five percent. When you greet a prospective customer or fellow worker/supervisor, let him feel your enthusiasm.

**Vintage Wisdom**

– Ron Blue (1942-)
Christian financial planner

## "Charitable giving should be a spiritual, rather than economic, decision. Economically, charitable giving never pays."

**(d)  Ask your immediate supervisor what you can do to improve the quality of the job you perform.** Be ready for his answer. Ask if you may request continuing advice as you seek to implement his suggestions.

**(e)  Be a life long learner and develop key skills.** Your continuing development as an employee is valuable whatever your line of work.

Ralph Waldo Emerson once said,

# "The difference between the person you are now and the person you will be in five years will be determined by the people you meet and the books you read."

**(f)  Meet as many successful people as possible in your field.** Ask their opinions. Aim to pick up one sales strategy or idea from each of these individuals you meet. Come up with five questions to ask them on how they would respond to certain situations or challenges. Develop your own suggestions. Most important, start receiving revelation about your job and how to maximize your effectiveness.

(g) **Renew your mind daily as you drive to work.** Pray that God will receive glory and honor from all you do. Pray about your attitude and thank God for the successful ideas He is giving you on becoming a better employee. Listen to Scripture, teaching, or worship tapes as you drive.

Treat the company as if it were you own. This applies to everything from picking up trash in hallways to looking for ways to increase overall productivity. When a fast-food employee gives you a handful of ketchup for your hamburger, both the boss and the buyer think it wasteful. A good employee is fair to both customer and company alike. If your company profits from good business, so will you.

— David Livingstone (1813-73)
Scottish missionary and explorer of Africa

**"I will place no value on anything I have or possess except in relation to the Kingdom of Christ. If anything I have will advance that Kingdom, it shall be given or kept whichever will best promote the glory of Him to whom I owe all my hopes, both for time and eternity."**

"You Can Have What You Want, But You Just Might **Lose** What You Have."

- Robb Thompson

# "Always Place Walls On Your Spending But Never Have A Ceiling On Your Income."

## – Robb Thompson

*Prosperity Pointer*

## Universal Truths Of Increase

### Jeremiah 31.27
"The time will come," says the Lord, "when I will greatly increase the population and multiply the number of cattle here in Israel and Judah."

### 2 Corinthians 9.10
Now He who supplies seed to the sower and bread for food will also supply and increase your store of seed and will enlarge the harvest of your righteousness.

No More Debt!

4056 7643 3782 2008

# Foreclose on DEBT- Fast And Forever!

# "Poor Decisions Forge The Links Of The Chain That Is Called Debt."

*– Robb Thompson*

In the richest society in world history, 80 million U.S. families would say that they are in financial trouble, after 50 years of almost unparalleled prosperity. Christians give 2.6 percent of their income to the cause of Christ, only slightly better than the total giving of those who deny Him. God's people globally control a majority of the world's wealth but spend 98 percent of those resources on themselves. Are our priorities in order? The answer is **NO!**

## Is Debt Really That Big Of A Problem? Take A Look At This...

**1. Credit Cards:** "About 10 percent of credit card holders had total card balances in excess of $10,000."

**2. Debt versus Income:** "More than a third—36 percent—of those who owe more than $10,000 on their cards have household incomes under $50,000."

**3. Rising Debt:** "The median value of total outstanding debt owed by homeowners rose 9.6 percent between 1998 and 2001."

**4. Bankruptcy:** "Bankruptcies set another record in 2003, with 1.6 million personal filings, the American Bankruptcy Institute reports." (*Four points taken from author Liz Pulliam Weston, The Truth about Credit Card Debt: Conventional Wisdom is That We're All Hooked and Struggling. MSN Money, May 8, 2006.*)

Never let yourself grow used to living with debt. I am not saying never borrow. You might need to at times. But never live with any load full term. That will help keep you debt free. Whenever you must borrow, always dedicate your energy and resources to repaying the loan as soon as possible. Never let debt become a lifestyle.

Just thirty years ago, only about 10 percent of individual earnings were being spent on consumer debt. Today, that figure has risen to a staggering 23 percent. That means almost one-fourth of the average person's earnings is now spent to service his ever-increasing debt!

Consumer debt grew by almost $100 billion in the twelve months of 1998. This amount brought the total to about $1 trillion! If this enormous debt were to be evenly divided among every man, woman, and child in the United States, they would each owe about $3,000. Now, mind you, that is only consumer debt. This figure does not include the more than $1 trillion

(1,000 billion) that the public owes to various lending institutions on their home mortgages.

## *A Cycle Of Defeat!*

Why do we do what we do?
**Think about this for a moment...**

Debt has become a ritual of maturity in America. Upon graduation from high school, parents proudly take their child down to the local bank. There they lovingly co-sign a loan for his very first car. With their action, they unwittingly launch him into his own ocean of red ink. Parents do this, sincerely believing they have given their child a real head start by establishing his credit rating early!

**That's crazy!** How much of a head start is this innocent child really receiving? He will probably begin his adulthood earning little more than minimum wage, yet he will owe the bank between five and fifteen thousand dollars on, of all things, a rapidly depreciating automobile!

This new debt has not helped him out one bit. Instead, his parents have just given their permission for the bank to hold their precious child in bondage. They have helped him pledge 1,000 to 3,000 hours of his life to serve the lender!

If what I am saying sounds too harsh, just think about it for a few minutes. **Remember, any truth that goes against common beliefs is never accepted easily.** Please keep your spirit open, and consider the entire matter before you react. I am teaching a tradition-breaking truth!

This young adult is now deeply indebted to the bank. He has promised to pay them a whopping twenty-five to seventy-five weeks of his pay. This represents six months or more of his meager wages. It is an obligation that can take as much as five years of his life to fulfill. If that's not a form of bondage, what is it?

# <u>DEBT</u> has reeked havoc on society and I must tell you: **It's not slowing down anytime soon!**

Experts tell us that today, as never before, our society is overwhelmed with anxiety. The greatest single reason for this emotional upheaval is attributable to money problems. The staggering debt with which most people are forced to live is more than their emotional systems were created to bear.

Please note that I am not speaking of financial deadbeats (those who borrow with no intention of repaying). I am speaking of good, honest people who have foolishly acquired more debt than they can repay. Our society is full of these folks. They suffer tremendous psychological pain. Their inability to manage their debts gives them a feeling of hopelessness.

More sleepless nights are attributed to unmanageable debt than to anything else. This debt has been largely responsible for America's becoming an around-the-clock society. Stores, television stations, and bars remain open twenty-four hours a day, primarily catering to the needs of the sleepless.

## 9 <u>Questions</u> to Ask Yourself Before Going into Debt

1. **Do I need it?** *(Colossians 3:15; Proverbs 1:5, 7; 20:27; 22:4)*
2. **How will it affect my wife? Husband? Children?** *(Amos 3:3; Proverbs 11:5, 12:15; Matthew 18:19)*
3. **Have I compared prices? Will its value rapidly increase or decrease?** *(Proverbs 13:16 AMP, 20:14, 27:23)*
4. **Will I want this item as much next week, next month, next year, as I do today?** *(Proverbs 27:12, 20; Ecclesiastes 3:1)*
5. **Will this purchase improve the quality of my life or that of my family?** *(Proverbs 11:2, 12:9, 26, 13:7, 10, 16:18)*
6. **Do I have a plan to repay this debt rapidly? Is the plan written out with timetables?** *(Proverbs 12:11, 27, 13:12, 21:5, 22:7; Hebrews 6:12)*
7. **Is this affordable in my present financial situation? Am I buying this only because it is on sale? Remember: If you really don't need it, it's not a good deal.** *(Proverbs 16:2-3, 21:20)*

8. **Have I considered the cost of owning this after I pay the price for getting it?** Can I maintain it? *(Luke 14:28; Proverbs 31:16)*

9. **Will this purchase help me in achieving God's goals for my life?** *(Proverbs 13:19, 19:21, 20:18).*

## Play With Debt And You Can Expect These 7 <u>Destructive</u> <u>Results</u>

**1. Debt contributes to divorce.**

Many Christians have a hard time believing God is concerned about their finances. Yet all Christians would agree that God has extreme concern for the sanctity of marriage. Well, beloved, here's a simple fact. Unmanageable debt is the leading cause of broken marriages! In a recent survey, over 60 percent of the 1.3 million newly divorced couples listed money (or more precisely, more debt than there was money to repay) as the main reason for their divorce.

With over 120,000 people going into bankruptcy or IVA every year, and upwards of one fifth of them divorcing or recently divorced, the 'grey area' between divorce and insolvency is effecting something like 30,000 families a year, adding further to their woes.

It's no wonder financial trouble is the leading cause of divorce. When debt is out of control, wives become afraid to answer the telephone. They fear hearing the harsh voice of another bill collector demanding payment. They are afraid to answer the door because they may be greeted by one of the utility companies that have come to shut off their service. Every time a truck pulls up on their street, they fear it is the man from the finance company coming to take back the television or the family car.

With a day of debt-induced terror behind her, you can easily imagine the warm greeting this housewife is going to give her already stressed-out husband when he walks in the door. Can you imagine the inadequate feelings the husband experiences as he listens to his wife's broken-hearted description of her day? Do you see how debt tears at marriage?

Christian marriages are not exempt! Husbands become threatened, even intimidated, when they fail to provide the basic necessities for their families. This lack strikes at the very essence of the husband's manhood.

## 2. Breadwinners become bread losers.

Even though many wives work outside the home, the husband is traditionally looked upon as the family's breadwinner. However, if he fails to provide adequate bread for the family, at least in his own mind, he becomes the family's bread loser. Financial failure causes him embarrassment, making him feel unattractive, even unworthy of his wife's attention. When the husband begins to feel inadequate in providing the basic necessities for his family, that family is well on its way to destruction.

The results are predictable. The most intimate relationships in that marriage start to fall apart. All meaningful communication stops as the relentless pressure of unpaid bills increases. Loving care is quickly replaced by short tempers. Family fights start over such things as whether or not it is really necessary to take Junior to the doctor. The real issue ceases to be if the child needs medical attention, but the underlying issue is, "How in the world will we be able to pay another doctor bill?"

**3. Families divide.**

The same tragic pattern often repeats itself among other family members. When son borrows from father, or when sister borrows from brother, and fails to pay back the debt, something much more serious than the loss of money takes place. Fathers and sons stop talking. Brothers and sisters cease to visit each other. In short, borrowing from relatives often results in a permanent breach in normal family relationships.

**4. Friendships collapse.**

Bad debts quickly break up lifelong friendships. When you borrow money from a friend, then cannot pay it back, what happens? Invariably, the friendship begins to weaken, then it just dies. If the amount of the debt was high enough, lifetime friends are turned into lifetime enemies.

## 5. Good employees become bad employees.

The pressures of unmanageable debt often trigger alcoholism and drug abuse. Previously good employees are driven to poor work habits, crime, or even suicide over their debt problems. Sleepless nights and meaningless days are the result of not being able to pay the bills. Eventually, a good employee becomes a bad one. Letters of commendation turn into warning notices, and eventually, the dreaded pink slip appears.

## 6. The Great Commission becomes the great omission.

The over-extended Christian can have little, if any, part in the Gospel outreach. Instead of his primary purpose being to reach the world for Christ, he must now allocate all his money to debt payments. To put it simply, his debt now rules him. He can no longer properly give to the cause of Christ. His new master will not let him. Debt always says no to the preaching of the Gospel. For all intents and purposes, the overburdened child of God has, by his own hand, cancelled his part in the Great Commission.

When the spirit of debt rules, the biggest goal the local church has is making the monthly mortgage payment. Satisfying the lender has replaced satisfying God. When this happens, the church is no longer the servant of God. Her own foolish actions have made her the servant of the lender.

Child of God, I hope the seriousness of this nightmare is beginning to sink into your spirit. Debt rules! Debt ruins!

Remember, the Word of God says: "…the borrower is servant to the lender" (*Proverbs 22:7).*

**7. Forced bankruptcy is just around the corner!**

When you come into uncontrollable debt, no financial decision can be made without first consulting your new ruler, the lender. You cannot go on vacation. You cannot buy desperately needed groceries for the hungry. You cannot even give to the Gospel.

## *"ROBB, WHAT ABOUT MY HOME…*
## *WHAT DO YOU SUGGEST?"*

The one material thing that Americans in particular have traditionally treasured through the decades is individual home ownership. Now the very homes that provide the foundation of the American dream, and in most cases, the primary source of financial security, are being placed in great jeopardy.

The American tradition has always been for a young couple to purchase a home so that in their senior years, the home is debt free. In the past, this plan has operated as a form of security for them in their retirement years, but not anymore. Instead, when the mortgage is paid down, the banks are now openly encouraging homeowners to borrow against their equity. Here is the shocking truth to this deception. Thirty percent of all home equity loans are used to repay other debts.

The federal government has actually helped encourage this type of borrowing, for home mortgage interest is one of the few tax deductions remaining for the average American.

Now the purchase of new cars or other high-ticket items is being called a "tax-smart move" when bought through second and third mortgages on the home. Financial planners and many tax experts recommend this type of purchase because the interests can still be deducted. As a result, home equity (retirement security) has little opportunity to build. The participant remains deep in debt for the entire span of his life. He never builds the much-needed retirement nest egg the debt-free home affords!

But, I am here to tell you that **YOU CAN HAVE A DEBT-FREE HOME!**

If you RESOLVE to pay off a mortgage as soon as possible, you can save many years and thousands of dollars off the traditional thirty-year home loan. The key to taking control of your mortgage is an unswerving determination that you absolutely will repay it in LESS than thirty years.

# 4 _Effective_ Strategies To Pay Off Your Mortgage

1. **The First-Day Payment Strategy.** This is one of the most powerful pre-payment tools. It quickly shrinks your loan balance and greatly shortens repayment time. Paying ahead always works well, but never better than when you make your first payment on the day the lender starts charging you interest. Every payment you make on the first day dramatically shortens your mortgage.

2. **The Split-Payment Strategy.** Another fast track to rapid mortgage payoff is to make a half payment every fourteen days (every two weeks). With this plan, each year you automatically make one extra payment and lower your principal balance twenty-six times instead of the standard twelve. This simple plan can take years off your mortgage and save you thousands of dollars in interest.

3. **The Specified Principal-Prepayment Strategy.** For this method you need an amortization schedule tailor-made to your mortgage. You must know exactly how much of each payment goes for the previous month's interest and how much is applied to your loan principal the next month. Here is this plan's secret. Adding next month's principal amount to this month's regular payment automatically cancels one whole payment from your loan!

4. **The Unspecified Principal-Reduction Strategy.** This has unlimited flexibility because it has no specified pre-payment amount. That can range from one cent over the regular payment up to the entire unpaid balance. It can be a one-time, monthly, or annual payment or a combination of these. You can add periodic bonuses or tax refunds to your regular payment. Every extra amount paid shortens the note term and reduces interest cost.

***Please note:*** You must make extra pay downs for any rapid debt-reduction strategy to work. When you make payments, do not write two checks. Add any extra amount to the check you would normally send.

## *"What about credit cards? Is it wrong for me to use credit cards?"*

First of all, let me clarify: Banks issue bankcards, not credit cards. Bankcards become credit cards when their users decide not to pay them off each month. Bankcards simply transfer funds electronically from the giver's bank to the receiver's bank. There is nothing wrong with using your bankcard as an electronic check. Just pay off the balance each month. Never use a bankcard as a quick loan. If you do, you will soon be paying 18 to 20 percent interest on the balance. "For which of you, intending to build a tower, sitteth not down first, and counteth the cost, whether he have sufficient to finish it?" (Luke 14:28). **Piling up costly credit card debt only leads to disaster.**

## *The Great Credit Card Dilemma...*

Holders of the first credit cards always had to pay off their balance each month. However, credit card companies eventually added the flexibility of a minimum payment. This led to vastly increased credit limits and installment purchasing without proper credit counseling.

As credit limits raised from only a few hundred dollars to several thousand, the every-growing monthly payment became a way of life. Now, borrowers could buy expensive items on impulse without payment planning.

This new kind of borrowing landed the final blow to the average individual's good budgeting habits. Loan firms began issuing credit cards to people without knowing their financial condition. Those with a fair credit rating and substantial incomes began finding "pre-approved" cards in the mailbox. Some of these cards came just days before the already over-extended recipient would have to begin missing payments on his other cards.

Now the recipient of these pre-approved cards could borrow against his cash allowance to pay the shortfall of his already overspent paycheck. This unsound spending soon has all credit cards charged to the limit, and bankruptcy becomes the next unavoidable step.

## *It's Time To Begin To Move Your Debt...*

Moving your consumer debts to the lowest available interest rate is a simple debt-reduction strategy. You can do this in several ways. Begin by checking with each lender who has issued you a credit card. Find out which card charges the lowest annual interest. Consider other fees – annual fees, transaction fees, etc. – that the lender charges.

If you still have unused credit available on the card with the lowest interest rate, transfer the debt from your highest-interest-rate credit card to it. Do this with all your cards until you have moved as much credit card debt as you can to the cards with the lowest interest rates. If you have a very-low-interest-rate card, ask this lender to extend your credit line to let you transfer more (or even all) of your other credit card debt to it.

## *The Key to Rapid Payoff...*

Keep your monthly payment at least as large as it was before you moved your debt. You will owe less interest and repay the principal faster. Always attack the smallest amount while paying the minimum on the other cards. After you take care of the smallest, apply that amount to the second smaller. And continue this until you take care of all of them.

## *3 Credit Card Tips*

1. **Know how your interest is figured if you plan to ever carry a balance.** Interest paid increases purchase cost.

2. **Never pay an annual fee.** Plenty of cards have none. If you pay one now, ask your credit card issuer to drop it. This works best if you have made your minimum monthly payments on time.

3. **Reduce your interest rate if it exceeds 16 percent.** Call your issuer today and ask that it be lowered. Most have a customer service 800 number. Due to competition, expect at least a 2 percent drop. Plenty of cards carry a rate of 14 percent or less, and your issuer knows it.

According to the Truth In Lending Act, all credit bills must be mailed at least 14 days in advance of the due date before finance and late charges can be added. Always save the envelope. The postmark will serve as proof if there is a dispute.

—Jesus
in Acts 20:35

Vintage Wisdom

**"It is more blessed to give than to receive."**

# *7 Practical <u>Steps</u> To Eliminate Your Debt*

1. **You Must Have A Workable Budget.** Not every budget fits everyone. You must find the one that you can effectively put into practice.

2. **Begin To Snowball Your Debt.** The principle is to stop everything except minimum payments and focus on one thing at a time. Otherwise, nothing gets accomplished because all your effort is diluted.

3. **Be Diligent, Disciplined, And Stubborn.** Don't deviate from your determination to eliminate any and all debt in your life.

4. **You Must Change Your Present Spending Habits.** You are a result of your habits. Don't think a budget will simply solve the problem. You must also change your wrong behavior when it comes to money.

5. **You Must Establish A Stable Savings Account.** Make sure you have an emergency fund (that you don't touch) and also a giving fund (where you build your giving resources).

6. **Focus On Your Future Pleasure, Not Your Present Pain.** Think about what you can do when you are debt free! Keep the goal in your mind. Don't allow yourself to focus on what you don't have. Think about where you are going.

7. **Focus On Sowing Your Seed To Overcome Your Need.** Have confidence in God's system. If He said it would work, then it will work. Don't worry when it seems to be taking a long time. It will happen and soon you will be debt free!

Let me give you one final principle as we start our journey toward being debt free!

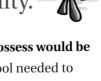

# Financial freedom often masks itself in fiscal stupidity.

**Money is not evil. If it were, any amount you possess would be wrong.** This lie causes many to reject the very tool needed to fulfill the Great Commission—"Go into the entire world and preach the Gospel." Now that takes money!

Always keep in mind these three important things:

- *God did not intend for anyone to live in continuous poverty, perpetual debt, or stubborn lack.*

- *God placed within us an inherent desire to prosper and brazenly excel.*

- *God gave us a desire to press beyond our present financial plateau.*

Therefore, we must rid ourselves of the thoughts that contradict God's Word. Although money doesn't produce happiness, what we can use it for does. Every time I sow into the Kingdom of God, joy floods my soul. I know that my money is some way helping another experience the love of God. Let us ask ourselves this profound question:

> **"How can I focus on meeting the needs of others when I am in debt and have no money to pay my own bills?"**

We are the engineers of our own prosperity. God shows us what we need to do to cultivate a prosperous life. It was never God's intention for mankind to live in poverty. What father would wish that upon his children? As we apply 2 Corinthians 9:6 and Joshua 1:8 to our lives, we soon make our way prosperous and we have good success.

— Charles Haddon Spurgeon (1834-92)
English Baptist preacher

## "Giving is true loving."

# "Action

**Is The 'Bridge'
That Links The
World Of Desire
With The Land
Of Fulfillment."**

*– Robb Thompson*

*Prosperity Pointer*

# "If You Are Not Committed To Creating Wealth, You Probably Won't."

## – Robb Thompson

## Universal Truths Of Increase

### Ecclesiastes 5.18-20

Even so, I have noticed one thing, at least, that is good. It is good for people to eat well, drink a good glass of wine, and enjoy their work—whatever they do under the sun—for however long God lets them live. And it is a good thing to receive wealth from God and the good health to enjoy it. To enjoy your work and accept your lot in life—that is indeed a gift from God. People who do this rarely look with sorrow on the past, for God has given them reasons for joy.

### Proverbs 13.21

Trouble chases sinners, while blessings chase the righteous!

# Negotiating An Operative Financial PLAN

# "The Planning Of Today Determines The Prosperity Of Tomorrow."

## — Robb Thompson

Understanding this principle of good planning is vital to the future progress of our lives. There are countless numbers of individuals who exist discontentedly because they're not where they wish to be. There are others, however, who experience great joy because they reap the rewards of the life they planned.

Additionally, far too many believers foolishly reject the interval of time when God attempts to lay the groundwork in order to decisively develop their character. This crucial season of planning is necessary to qualify them for what God desires them to accomplish.

Like the computer company executive who skillfully devised a stratagem, we cannot afford to neglect to plan for our future. What type of builder would attempt to build a skyscraper without first having a blueprint? Why is it any different when building a life? God wants to bring all of us a great future, but only those who plan will ever experience it. Although opportunity may come to all, only those who ready themselves can recognize that opportunity when it lands upon their own threshold. Take time now to develop a plan to attain the future you desire. Now is a great time to formulate a sweeping plan.

# A great future requires a detailed map.

God does nothing without first laying out a detailed plan. Proverbs tells us, "A man's heart plans his way, but the Lord directs his steps." God is into details.

When we are committed to our dream and express it with a detailed plan of carrying it out, we provide ourselves with a visual reminder of where we are going, and how we believe we will arrive there. The journey of life always starts with a vision, but too many individuals stop right there, parking as if permanently stationed in the lot of a supermarket. They go no farther than the vision. We must understand that every journey has great costs associated with it. These costs may be in terms of time, energy, finances, choices, sacrifices, and a number of other factors.

We must begin to take the vision we have for our lives and carefully write it out, making it plain before our eyes. As we do, God begins to birth within us a roadmap that will give us the necessary directions to fulfill what He assigned us to do. Without a detailed plan of action, our destinies are never reached; but with it, our lives become a dream come true.

# A plan is the roadmap that takes you along the journey of life.

Often, people ask me, "What is the best way to turn my debt into wealth?" My simple response is: **Strategic planning.**

Strategic planning (or a life plan) enables you to turn your dreams into reality by defining specific, measurable steps of progress, along with precise beginnings and endings. If you wanted to drive to another state, you would need a map or a specific route to get there. Although that map is not able to foretell any obstacles, detours, or potholes, it gives you criteria to follow.

At some time or another, you may have used an electronic mapping system. By entering your present location and your desired destination, it provides your best route. And that's the precise purpose of a life plan. Why?

# A plan bridges the gap between what you desire and its fulfillment.

Do you remember the case of the prominent engineer who lacked specific blueprints to build the skyscraper? Allow me to say it again: All wealthy individuals operate from a written plan. Additionally, most great achievements were preceded and accompanied by a detailed plan, carefully designed and calculated from beginning to end.

# Without such a plan, <u>NO</u> dream ever becomes a reality. Once you have a clear sense of your purpose, you must be prepared to start working on your plan.

Now I can hear some of you asking, "How do I put together such a plan?" First, you must determine where every dollar is going to go at the beginning of each month. Give each dollar an assignment before you are able to spend it.

Let's say you've decided to map out your health goals. In this case, you must carefully determine what kind of eating lifestyle you want, how much you will exercise, and the proper rest you will need to accomplish that particular goal.

As you utilize a strategic plan in each area of your life, you'll begin to notice how clear your life will eventually become.

Habitual behavior is the reason some succeed where others fail. What you do consistently is what matters. I like to say it like this: Winners do regularly what failures do rarely.

## AVOID the 5 <u>Enemies</u> of Planned Spending

1.  **Don't develop a penny pincher mentality.** If there is no allowance for pleasure, the plan is doomed from the start. Plan a family reward when the goal is met or schedule a pleasurable time together. Without a planned reward, a splurge will bring guilt and make the spending plan look like a failure.

2.  **Work together in the plan.** Get your spouse's input. It is important to work together.

3.  **Avoid the gratification syndrome.** Realize people sometimes use money as a cure for feeling low or a reward for a job well done. Keep sight of your goal.

4.  **Don't allow money to replace self-esteem.** Some people "pick up the tab" or do other things not in their budget to "appear" in good shape.

5.  **It's foolish to give unless God is in it.** "Give and it shall be given unto you; good measure, pressed down, and shaken together, and running over, shall men give into your bosom" *(Luke 6:38)*.

God has given each of us the power to get wealth. Power means strength or might. The Bible teaches that all real power comes from God, but He chooses to use ordinary people like you and me.

What do you need to tap into this "**POWER**"?

**P** – Plan

**O** – Organization

**W** – Work

**E** – Enthusiasm

**R** – Reward

### *Plan*

In Greek and Aramaic, a plan is a thought, decision, or purpose. "The plans of the diligent lead surely to plenty, but those of everyone who is hasty, surely to poverty" (Proverbs 21:5 NKJV). To succeed, you must have a goal. Plans give you power!

### *Organization*

1. **Develop short-term** (next twelve months) **and long-term** (next five years) **goals in the spiritual, familial, financial, mental, social, and physical areas of your life.**
2. **Write a plan to reach each goal.**

3. Write a specific timetable for taking each step.
4. Regularly check progress in each area. Organization means power!

## Work

Lasting wealth only comes through God-inspired work. Work is anything accomplished by hand, art, industry, or mind. In other words, work is implementing your plans.

Proverbs 13:11 says, "Wealth [not earned but] won in haste or unjustly or from the production of things for vain or detrimental use [such riches] will dwindle away, but he who gathers little by little will increase [his riches]."

Plan, organize well, and begin to work your plan. Work is power!

## Enthusiasm

Be sold on what you are doing.

## Rewards

Reward means dues paid for work. God will reward us for our good endeavors. You can achieve the reward of wealth with proper planning, good organization, diligent work, and enthusiasm.

Remember, there are **NO** get-rich-quick gimmicks – **NO** daily doubles – to getting wealth. There is **ONLY** the power God gave you to get wealth.

# "Every Failure In Life Can Be Traced Back To A Compromise In Character."

– Robb Thompson

# "Obedience Is The Master Key That Unlocks Heaven's Abundance."

## – *Robb Thompson*

## Universal Truths Of Increase

### *Luke 5.5-7*
"Master," Simon replied, "we worked hard all last night and didn't catch a thing. But if You say so, we'll try again." And this time their nets were so full they began to tear! A shout for help brought their partners in the other boat, and soon both boats were filled with fish and on the verge of sinking.

### *3 John 1.2*
Dear friend, I am praying that all is well with you and that your body is as healthy as I know your soul is.

# OBEDIENCE:
# Zoning In
# On God's
# Abundance

# "The Greatest Seed Of Man Is The Seed Of Obedience To God."

*– Robb Thompson*

God searches the earth, looking for someone upon whom He can shower His blessings. God is a good God and desires to bless His children. We must understand, however, that God does not reward disobedience. We can see throughout all of Scripture how God resists those who choose the route of disobedience and rebellion.

The greatest pleasure Heaven ever receives is to be believed. If we want to please God and receive the rewards He has for us, we must choose to obey.

 There is no greater proof that we believe the Word of God than obedience to it.

The greatest seed one can ever sow is the seed of obedience...it harvests an abundant crop of reward. James exhorts us with

these words, "…being not a heedless listener who forgets but an active doer [who obeys], he shall be blessed in his doing (his life of obedience)." The life we desire lies within the seed of our obedience.

## 9 <u>Important</u> Keys Of Obedience

1. **One's Enjoyment In Life Is In Direct Proportion To His Or Her Commitment To Divine Principles.**

   - *Where does your commitment lie with God?*

   - *If there were to be a trial, would you be found guilty of a life committed to God?*

These are two questions we must ask ourselves if we truly want to enjoy life. Jesus told us, "I come to give life and life more abundant."

Do we want that kind of life? It won't come to just anyone… there is a requirement.

**You must commit your life to Christ Jesus. He must reign (like a king reigns over a nation) as Lord in your heart, directing your every decision.**

Our commitment to God goes no deeper than our commitment to His Word. There are believers who claim they are committed to God but refuse to do what God commands in His Word. Jesus says, "Why do you call Me, 'Lord, Lord,' and do not what I said?"

Though many Jewish priests were committed to studying the Scriptures, during His ministry, Jesus told the Pharisees, "You honor Me with your lips, but your hearts are full of all kinds of evil." Your commitment to God is proven through your passionate pursuit of obeying His Word. It must be your greatest desire. If you ever truly want to enjoy life, obedience is the safest and best route to take. It may just be the only route you can take.

## 2. God's Will Can Only Be Discovered On The Road Of Obedience.

I hear it quite frequently, "What is God's will for my life?" All of us want to know what career we are to pursue, who we are to marry, and where we are to live. But we must understand that only those who choose to travel upon the road of obedience will discover God's unknown will. God called humanity to simply obey; it is His will for our lives. As John the Baptist walked down the highway of obedience, and Jesus walked upon the road of obedience, we too must submit ourselves to the instructions that lie within the pages of God's written Word, putting a sound conclusion to infinite searching and exhaustive wondering.

# Jesus came with one purpose: To **OBEY** the instructions of His Father.

Our calling in life is to please the One who chose us. When we focus upon obeying the Word of God, we no longer are distracted with the perpetual curiosity of God's unknown will. As we obey, we are assured that He leads and guides our steps.

It is only a matter of time before we enter His perfect will for our lives. Let us renew our minds to the call that is placed upon our lives to passionately obey God's known will—His written Word.

3.  **The Main Ingredient To Enjoying The Rewards Of Life Is Genuine Compliance.**

Obedience simply means doing what God instructs us in His Word. It means to live up to the knowledge we receive. God told Abram, "Abram, I want you to move from your comfortable situation and go to a new country." Abram obeyed God. If God talks to us about something, we must do it. Our Heavenly Father expects each of His children to yield to Him with wholehearted obedience.

# The entrance into this new life with Christ demands the vow of absolute <u>OBEDIENCE</u>.

As Christians, we must surrender our whole being, exactly as Jesus did, to be, think, speak, and act according to the will of God; it is not enough to just agree with Him. It is only through obedience that our agreement is proven, and in doing so, we have access to God's favor and abundant blessings. As Jesus continued His sermon, distinct commands were given. Instructions such as:

- *Rejoice and be exceedingly glad when persecuted.*

- *You are the salt of the world so don't lose your flavor.*

- *You are the light of the world so don't hide your light.*

- *You know it's not right to kill, but neither should you be angry without cause.*

Jesus knew that God requires obedience. Every act of our obedience is an added ingredient unto a just reward. Jesus said in Matthew 7:21 that obedience is the very essence of salvation. Obedience opens the door to all God has to give—most importantly, an intimate relationship with God Himself.

4. **The Greatest Responsibility Placed Upon Any Man Is Adherence To The Word Of God.**

In a southern California city is a glamorous movie theatre whose towering spotlight flickers and floats across the desert sky, drawing people to its nightly showings. That spotlight is proof something is going on.

Our unwavering obedience and positive attitude draw Heaven's spotlight—proof that something exciting is going on—not in some old movie theatre, but inside the hearts of His people! The Bible never says, "If you love Me, you will eat the best of the land." It says, "If you are willing and obedient, you shall eat the best of the land."

Our obedience is the only proof that we trust God. The success of our life by Heaven's standards depends on our obedience to the written Word of God. The more accurately we obey, the greater the rewards.

<u>Picture this:</u> A mother asks her son to take care of the dishes while she is out. She comes home to find a beautiful bouquet of flowers, a sweet "I Love You" card, and a sink full of dirty dishes. Is she to believe her son loves her because of the flowers and card? Perhaps, if he did the dishes, but his disobedience to her specific instruction speaks louder than the sacrifice he went through to buy the flowers and the card.

## **<u>OBEDIENCE</u>** is better than sacrifice.

Solomon had everything, yet in Ecclesiastes 12:13 he came to one conclusion: Fear God and obey His commands.

# **OBEDIENCE** to the Word of God is the one responsibility for which every man has to give an account on the Day of Judgment.

God places such a high emphasis on obedience because our actions prove exactly who we are.

5. **Only The Obedient Are Invited To Attend The Banquet Of Reward.**

**So many choices...**
- A **movie** or a **move** of God through sacrificial prayer?
- Support of a new missionary **outreach** or the purchase of another new **outfit**?

One of the greatest gifts anyone could ever receive is the power of choice. God gave us the ability to create our future. Whether it is prosperous or disastrous, the choice is ours. The apostle Paul encourages us with these words, "For God is working in you, giving you the desire to obey Him and the power to do what pleases Him." God doesn't just leave us as orphans to fend for ourselves. He knows there is an enemy out there whose sole purpose is to lure us into making wrong choices. If Satan causes us to make just one mistake, it may result in a lifetime of negative consequences.

We can see throughout the Scriptures that God did not predestine our choices. He did, however, predestine our consequences. We are to surrender our lives to the Spirit of God and trust in Him to help us make right choices.

The Holy Spirit is our helper; He guides us in the right direction.

As all of us know for certain—**the <u>rewards</u> of obedience far outweigh the consequences of disobedience.**

6. **Obedience To The Voice Of God Is Dependent Upon Our Character, Not Our Circumstances.**

We are distinctly called to walk by faith, not by what we mistakenly perceive with our senses. God speaks only truth because it is impossible for Him to lie. His Word is His bond. He doesn't say one thing and then do another. What He said must become the final word even in the midst of very challenging circumstances.

Oftentimes, we declare that God is a liar by our reaction to the circumstances in which we find ourselves. What we see is temporal, but what we don't see (the promises of God's Word) is eternal. Choosing to live by the unseen promises of God guarantees a life that is built on a solid foundation.

### 7. Genuine Obedience Begins In Your Heart Before It Ever Finds Its Way Into Your Actions.

Jesus told the story of two boys who were given an instruction. One said he would do it, and never did. The other said he wouldn't do what he was asked, but shortly afterwards, he felt conviction in his heart and completed the instruction. Even though this boy denied the instruction with his lips, his sense of obedience permeated all the way to his heart. From there, he went to work, and no doubt afterwards, he returned to his father to inform him that he had indeed obeyed.

I believe very strongly in voicing our desire to obey, but I believe even more strongly in putting our obedience into action. If you are a believer, God gave you a new heart that really desires to obey.

We must, at all cost, go to battle against this trio of pride, bitterness, and offense to rescue the obedient heart God gave us. Then, we can get to work with our instructions, both from men and from Heaven. And last, we can say, "I obeyed."

### 8. The Fragrance That Pleases God Is The Aroma Of Your Hourly Obedience.

Obedience is the only thing God ever explicitly requires. Although a faithful and loving God, precious few are quick to obey His instructions. On occasion, what God tells us may seem utterly illogical, or brutally disappointing. It may also, at diverse times, keep us from getting something we desire. Yet, it is not until we obey Him without restraint that our obedience infiltrates Heaven with its pleasant aroma.

The apostle Paul instructs us to "present our bodies a living sacrifice, holy, acceptable to God, which is our reasonable service."

# We must give up claim to our childish wants, individual desires, and selfish reasoning so we can stalwartly <u>OBEY</u> the Lord.

God delights in our obedience, and requires us to conform to His instruction. The obedience we offer Him far exceeds our daily sacrifice, since God does not ask us to make a grand sacrifice; He simply requests daily obedience in the little things. That is the only sacrifice He is pleased to accept; it is the way He crafted us.

9. **Obedience Is The Only Evidence Necessary In The Courtroom Of Heaven To Prove Your Love For God.**

How can we say we love God, but deliberately neglect the things He instructs us to do—like love one another and completely forsake care and worry? We must understand that God is the One who adequately determines whether or not we truly love

Him. God made it clear to us that He wants us to show His love to others, not only through the words that we speak, but also through the actions we perform.

When we leave the futile realm of insincere words and move into the mode of obedience is when Heaven and earth know we love God. Obedience was foremost in Jesus' mind at the final Passover before His death. It was the only evidence necessary for God's plan of redemption to continue, and Jesus Himself confirmed it saying, "So that the world may know that I love the Father, I do as He commanded." As we begin to do what God commanded, we soon have enough evidence to bring before the courtroom of Heaven to prove we truly love God.

## 3 *Fatal Enemies* Of Obedience

### 1. PRIDE

Since Adam and Eve sinned, all of humanity has been infected with pride, contaminated as bleakly as a garden of wilted leaves. However, there is wonderful news: Christ came to cure us of that infection, which even caused Satan to be ousted from the magnificent splendors of Heaven. But how are we to conquer pride in our lives, once and for all? Well, there are two things we must do.

**First**, we must humble ourselves, becoming as meek as young children.

**Second**, we must willingly accomplish exactly what God called us to complete. As we continually place ourselves under His mighty hand, eventually, we will be exalted.

Prideful people customarily demand respect and admiration, but respect that is demanded is not true respect. You see, just as a doctor must earn his license in order to practice medicine, true respect also must be earned.

**Humility**—do you realize that is the highest virtue any man can possess? God's Word continually tells us to humble ourselves; Jesus is our prime example. The apostle Paul explains it in Philippians 2:8, "And being found in appearance as a man, He humbled Himself and became obedient to the point of death." The Son of God became a human to save all of humanity. What greater example do we need?

Jesus was highly exalted and obtained a name that is above every other name. Likewise, we must humble ourselves as children today, in order to be exalted as praiseworthy men and women in the future.

## 2. BITTERNESS

The bitter herb found on the Seder plate (usually foul-smelling horseradish) helps Jews around the world deal with the remembrance of the bitter things that happened before and during their flight from Egypt. One of the most effective weapons hell possesses is bitterness.

God gave us the mighty weapon of forgiveness to combat bitterness.

> **BITTERNESS** wipes the smile from the heart and siphons passion from someone who desires to serve God and love His people.

It paralyzes the gifts and abilities God placed within us. In order to experience true happiness, we must overcome any offense Satan brings our way. People will utter unkind words concerning us, hurt us, and even betray us. Yet, we must respond in faith and forgive anyone who wrongs us.

# Through **FORGIVENESS**,
# we defeat the power of bitterness,
# conquering it once and for all.

Understanding how much Jesus forgave us is crucial when it comes to us forgiving others. We cannot afford to harbor offense within our hearts. Un-forgiveness leads to sickness and disease within our bodies.

We must be quick to follow the words of the apostle Paul, "Let all bitterness, and wrath, and anger, and clamor, and evil speaking, be put away from you, with all malice: and be kind one to another, tenderhearted, forgiving one another, even as God for Christ's sake hath forgiven you" (Ephesians 4:31-32). By following this instruction to forgive, we can walk free from bitterness (and its foul smell) and live tenderhearted, peaceable lives.

## 3. OFFENSE

What could possibly be a greater reason to get offended than being hunted by the one you are trying to serve? David gave his life for the king's service—he served faithfully in the army and loyally in the palace. In everything he did, his heart was toward Saul, and for Saul's prosperous reign. Never did he see himself as the one who should be king in Saul's place, though he knew very well that one day such would be the case.

# He entrusted himself to the hand of God, who always judges justly, and who sets kings on thrones or removes them from power.

While in the wilderness, the Jews were in constant offense. Sometimes it was Moses. Sometimes it was their environment. And most often it was God. They literally breathed an atmosphere of wretched offense.

Do you or I have any reason to get offended in light of what David endured? Have we left our family and all our desires for another's sake?

And have we, in turn, been hunted unto death? Of course not! What kept David from being offended with Saul? It was his purity of heart—he wanted what was best for the king, not what he could get from the king. If we develop that heart toward the people around us, especially our superiors, we won't have further bouts with offense.

# "Honor

## Is The Doorway Through Which All Prosperity Walks."

*– Robb Thompson*

# "The Steady Paycheck That Produces Comfort And Security Is Also The One That May Keep You From Ever Achieving Your Potential."

## – Robb Thompson

*Prosperity Pointer*

## Universal Truths Of Increase

### Zechariah 9.17

How wonderful and beautiful they will be! The young men and women will thrive on the abundance of grain and new wine.

### Proverbs 15.6

There is treasure in the house of the godly, but the earnings of the wicked bring trouble.

# Money
# Bag Section

# *Confession Scriptures For Prosperity*

## Genesis 8:22

*While the earth remaineth, seedtime and harvest, and cold and heat, and summer and winter, and day and night shall not cease.*

**Father, I want to thank You for Your covenant and I know that as long as my life remains, I will use the principle of seedtime and harvest to produce an abundant crop for Your purposes on the earth.**

## Deuteronomy 8:18

*But thou shalt remember the Lord thy God: for it is He that giveth thee power to get wealth, that He may establish His covenant which He sware unto thy fathers, as it is this day.*

**Father, I thank You that You have given me the power to get wealth that You may establish Your covenant on the earth through me.**

## Deuteronomy 29:9

*Keep therefore the words of this covenant, and do them, that ye may prosper in all that ye do.*

**Father, I keep the words of Your covenant and I thank You for causing me to prosper in all that I do.**

## Deuteronomy 14:22

*Thou shalt truly tithe all the increase of thy seed, that the field bringeth forth year by year.*

**Father, I am a tither and I thank You for increasing my seed so I can sow more, and thank You for causing me to have an abundant harvest every year.**

## Deuteronomy 16:15b

*…because the Lord thy God shall bless thee in all thine increase, and in all the works of thine hands, therefore thou shalt surely rejoice.*

**Father, I thank You that You cause me to rejoice for You bless me and cause me to increase in all the work of my hands.**

## Deuteronomy 28:2

*And all these blessings shall come upon thee, and overtake thee, if thou shalt hearken diligently unto the voice of the Lord thy God.*

**Father, I hearken unto Your voice and I thank You that all Your blessings come upon me and overtake me.**

## Romans 8:32

*He that spared not His own Son, but delivered Him up for us all, how shall He not with Him also freely give us all things?*

**Father, I thank You because You did not spare Your own Son but gave Him up for us all, and You lavishly bestow upon me all things freely.**

## Proverbs 8:12

*I wisdom dwell with prudence, and find out knowledge of witty inventions.*

> **Father, thank You for blessing me with wisdom and prudence and revealing to me Your witty inventions.**

## Joshua 1:7

*Only be thou strong and very courageous, that thou mayest observe to do according to all the law, which Moses My servant commanded thee: turn not from it to the right hand or to the left, that thou mayest prosper whithersoever thou goest.*

> **Father, I am strong and courageous. I walk by faith and not by sight. I will not turn from Your Word for it causes me to prosper in whatever I do.**

## Malachi 3:10

*Bring ye all the tithes into the storehouse, that there may be meat in Mine house, and prove Me now herewith, saith the Lord of hosts, if I will not open you the windows of heaven, and pour you out a blessing, that there shall not be room enough to receive it.*

> **I am a tither. I bring all my tithes into the storehouse so God can have provision in His house. This is my way of proving God. I decree this day that He opens the windows of heaven and pours out blessings upon me that I do not have room enough to receive.**

## Joshua 1:8

_This book of the law shall not depart out of thy mouth; but thou shalt meditate therein day and night, that thou mayest observe to do according to all that is written therein: for then thou shalt make thy way prosperous, and then thou shalt have good success._

**This book of God's Word will not depart out of my mouth, but I will meditate on it day and night. I will observe to do according to all that is written therein, for then I will make my way prosperous, and then I will have good success.**

## 1 Chronicles 4:9-10

_Now Jabez was more honorable than his brothers, and his mother called his name Jabez, saying, "Because I bore him in pain." And Jabez called on the God of Israel saying, "Oh, that You would bless me indeed, and enlarge my territory, that Your hand would be with me, and that You would keep me from evil, that I may not cause pain!" So God granted him what he requested. NKJV_

**Father, I thank You that You bless me indeed and enlarge my substance, that Your hand is upon me, that You keep me from evil, and that I will not cause anyone any pain.**

## Job 36:11

_If they obey and serve Him, they shall spend their days in prosperity, and their years in pleasures._

**I serve the Lord my God in obedience and I spend my days in prosperity, and my years are spent in pleasures.**

## Psalm 1:1-3

*Blessed is the man that walketh not in the counsel of the ungodly, nor standeth in the way of sinners, nor sitteth in the seat of the scornful. But his delight is in the law of the Lord; and in His law doth he meditate day and night. And he shall be like a tree planted by the rivers of water, that bringeth forth his fruit in his season; his leaf also shall not wither; and whatsoever he doeth shall prosper.*

**Father, I thank You that I do not walk in the counsel of the ungodly nor do I stand in the path of sinners, nor do I sit in the seat of the scornful. But my delight and desire is in Your Word and in Your Word do I habitually meditate, ponder, and orally recite it both day and night. And I am like a tree that is planted by the rivers of water, and I bring forth my fruit in its right seasons. And my leaf also shall not whither and whatever I put my hand to shall prosper.**

## Proverbs 11:24-25

*There is that scattereth, and yet increaseth; and there is that withholdeth more than is meet, but it tendeth to poverty. The liberal soul shall be made fat: and he that watereth shall be watered also himself.*

**Father, I scatter and I continue to increase. I never withhold more than I should and I will not be led to poverty. I have a liberal soul and it will be made fat, and I will water others and I myself also will be watered.**

## Psalm 35:27

_Let them shout for joy, and be glad, that favour My righteous cause: yea, let them say continually, Let the Lord be magnified, which hath pleasure in the prosperity of His servant._

**Father, I shout for joy and I am glad for I favor Your righteous cause. I say continually, "Let the Lord be magnified because He has pleasure in my prosperity."**

## Psalm 84:11

_For the Lord God is a sun and shield: the Lord will give grace and glory: no good thing will He withhold from them that walk uprightly._

**Lord, I thank You for being my sun and shield. You have given me grace and glory. There is no good thing that You will withhold from me because I will walk uprightly.**

## 2 Corinthians 9:6-7

_But this I say: He who sows sparingly will also reap sparingly, and he who sows bountifully will also reap bountifully. So let each one give as he purposes in his heart, not grudgingly or of necessity; for God loves a cheerful giver._

**Father, I will always remember that a farmer who plants only a few seeds will get a small crop, but I choose to plant generously and I will receive a generous crop. I have already made up my mind to be an abundant sower, not reluctantly or in response to pressure, but because You love me, a cheerful giver.**

## Proverbs 8:20-21

*I lead in the way of righteousness, in the midst of the paths of judgment: that I may cause those that love Me to inherit substance; and I will fill their treasures.*

**My Father, I love Your truth; it leads me in the way of righteousness and causes me to walk in the paths of good judgment. Your truth causes me to inherit wealth and it fills my treasuries.**

## Psalm 122:6

*Pray for the peace of Jerusalem: they shall prosper that love thee.*

**Father, I thank You for the peace of Jerusalem and I thank You for prospering me because of my love for her.**

## Psalm 85:12

*Yea, the Lord shall give that which is good; and our land shall yield her increase.*

**The Lord gives me the good of the land and causes me to increase.**

## Proverbs 10:22

*The blessing of the Lord, it maketh rich, and He addeth no sorrow with it.*

**Father, I thank You that Your blessing makes me rich and You add no sorrow to me.**

## Proverbs 3:9-10

*Honour the Lord with thy substance, and with the firstfruits of all thine increase: so shall thy barns be filled with plenty, and thy vats shall burst out with new wine.*

**I honor the Lord with my wealth and with the first fruits of all my increase. My barns will be filled with plenty and my vats will brim over with new wine.**

## Proverbs 18:20

*A man's belly shall be satisfied with the fruit of his mouth; and with the increase of his lips shall he be filled.*

**Father, I know that my words satisfy my soul as food satisfies my stomach and my right words cause me to greatly increase.**

## Proverbs 30:7-8

*Two things have I required of Thee; deny me them not before I die: remove far from me vanity and lies: give me neither poverty nor riches; feed me with food convenient for me:*

**My Father, I require two things of You while I live: remove falsehood and lies far from me and give me neither poverty nor riches, but feed me with the food that You prescribe for me.**

## Matthew 6:33

*But seek ye first the kingdom of God, and His righteousness; and all these things shall be added unto you.*

**Father, I thank You that because I seek Your kingdom and Your righteousness first and foremost in my life, all things of life are added to me.**

## Isaiah 55:8-11

*For My thoughts are not your thoughts, neither are your ways My ways, saith the Lord. For as the heavens are higher than the earth, so are My ways higher than your ways, and My thoughts than your thoughts. For as the rain cometh down, and the snow from heaven, and returneth not thither, but watereth the earth, and maketh it bring forth and bud, that it may give seed to the sower, and bread to the eater: so shall My Word be that goeth forth out of My mouth: it shall not return unto Me void, but it shall accomplish that which I please, and it shall prosper in the thing whereto I sent it.*

**Father, I thank You for the opportunity to exchange my thoughts for Your Word, and I allow Your ways to take the place of my ways. My words are taken from Your Word; therefore, I speak as You speak. Your Word comes to pass in my life and You cause me to prosper in every area.**

## 2 Corinthians 9:10

*Now He that ministereth seed to the sower both minister bread for your food, and multiply your seed sown, and increase the fruits of your righteousness.*

> **Father, I thank You for providing me seed to sow and bread for my food, that You multiply my seed sown, and that You continually increase the fruits of my righteousness.**

## Luke 6:38

*Give, and it shall be given unto you; good measure, pressed down, and shaken together, and running over, shall men give into your bosom. For with the same measure that ye mete withal it shall be measured to you again.*

> **I give and it is given unto me. Good measure, pressed down, shaken together, and running over shall men give unto me.**

## 1 Corinthians 3:7

*So then neither is he that planteth any thing, neither he that watereth; but God that giveth the increase.*

> **Father, I thank You that because I have planted, You now abundantly provide the increase.**

## 3 John 2

*Beloved, I wish above all things that thou mayest prosper and be in health, even as thy soul prospereth.*

**Father, I thank You that Your greatest desire for me is that I would prosper and be in health because my soul is prospering.**

## Philippians 4:19

*But my God shall supply all your need according to His riches in glory by Christ Jesus.*

**Father, I thank You that You will supply all of my needs according to Your riches in glory by Christ Jesus.**

## 2 Corinthians 8:9

*For ye know the grace of our Lord Jesus Christ, that, though He was rich, yet for your sakes He became poor, that ye through His poverty might be rich.*

**For I know the grace of my Lord and Savior, Jesus Christ, that though He was rich, yet for my sake He became poor, so that I through His poverty might become rich.**

## Galatians 6:7-9

*Do not be deceived, God is not mocked; for whatever a man sows, that he will also reap. For he who sows to his flesh will of the flesh reap corruption, but he who sows to the Spirit will of the Spirit reap everlasting life. And let us not grow weary while doing good, for in due season we shall reap if we do not lose heart.*

**Father, I refuse to be deceived; I will not make a fool of You. For I know that whatever I sow, that is what I am going to reap. If I sow to my flesh, I will reap corruption from my flesh. But I will sow to my spirit and I will reap everlasting life. And I do not grow weary in well doing, for unless I throw in my hand, my ultimate harvest is assured.**

# *29 <u>SILLY</u> Ways To Burn Money!*

1. Borrowing money on your credit cards.

2. Paying credit card annual fees, especially higher gold card fees. You keep the card; "they" take your gold.

3. Buying lottery tickets.

4. Maintaining low deductibles on your property and casualty policies (auto; homeowners, etc.).

5. Wasting postage stamps on Publisher's Clearinghouse.

6. Subscribing to premium cable television services, such as HBO, Showtime, etc. or any pay-per-view event.

7. Specialty insurance policies such as: cancer, life insurance on children, etc.

8. Ordering a TV-offer get rich package "revealing" how to become a real estate millionaire over night.

9. Buying anything from television home shopping programs.

10. Buying a time-share vacation package before figuring out what this "deal" really costs.

11. Paying for a television guide when they are free in your local newspaper.

12. Using an ATM that costs money when you can plan ahead and withdraw money or use a check.

13. Donating over the phone to anyone who is unfamiliar.

14. Joining in a chain letter or get-rich-quick scheme offered by your "friends."

15. Investing money by phone with a stranger.

16. Buying anything from someone just because they are a "friend."

17. Buying a boat or recreational vehicle.

18. Buying a new or pre-owned car without a definite purchase price in mind.

19. Eating at fast-food restaurants.

20. Buying name brand food, beauty, and household products.

21. Loaning money to family or friends.

22. Buying designer clothes at expensive department stores.

23. Subscribing to magazines you don't read.

24. Buying goods or services just because they are on sale.

25. Not using coupons.

26. Buying drinks at the fast-food drive through.

27. Carrying lots of cash. Spending is too easy.

28. Making long-distance calls during peak-cost times.

29. Going grocery shopping while you are hungry.

"The Instant You Achieve Prosperity Is The Instant

# Money

Is No Longer The Driving Force Behind Your Decisions... PASSION Is..."

*- Robb Thompson*

# 7 Practical <u>Tips</u> On How To Sell A Home Rapidly

Sometimes your rapid debt reduction strategy may call for the sale of your present house so that you can move to a home you can afford. In the following pages, you will find some helpful ideas for selling at a reasonable price in the shortest possible time.

## 1. Choose the Right Representative

It is usually easier for a realtor to sell your home than for you to sell it on your own. There are certain sales tools available to him that are not available to you. He has access to multiple listing services as well as other advertising methods. The dollars you spend on a good realtor's commission will be will worth it if he effects a fast sale at a fair price.

## 2. Your Agency should know Your Area

Your first priority in choosing the right company to represent you is to find an agency that has successfully sold other homes in your neighborhood. A little investigation will tell you which agents have made the most sales in your area in recent months. Remember, what you want is a go-getter who will work for you.

The more your agent knows about your particular area, the better. He should be able to tell prospective buyers about schools, churches, stores, parks, and a number of other things in your community. The realtor must be sold on your neighborhood before he can sell it to someone else. He should feel that your house is a good buy for anyone who fits into your price range.

### 3. Overpriced Means Overlooked

Remember, today's buyers are looking for a good deal. Your home won't sell if you are asking too much for it. Let your agent help you figure out a realistic selling price; comparing recent sales in your area will accomplish this. There are dependable, mathematical formulas that will tell you how much your house should sell for. If you have a reputable realtor, you can trust the sale price he suggests.

### 4. A Few Dollars Spent Will Bring Big Money

You should be prepared to spend a little money to make your house stand out. It will cost you only three or four hundred dollars to make a real difference in your home's eye appeal. How your house looks from the curb can make a real difference to the buyer.

Touch up the outside paint, especially the trim. Wash the windows, and patch up cracks in the driveway and walkways. Be sure your yard is cleaned up and freshly mowed. Rake up the

leaves, and clean leaves and other debris out of the gutter. If you have hedges, be sure they are neatly trimmed. Planting a few flowers along the walkway or around trees, or putting potted flowers on the porch, will enhance the outside appearance tremendously.

## 5. Cleanliness Says, "Buy Me"

Do a major cleaning on the inside of the house. Your house makes a distinctive impression when the kitchen and bathrooms are spotless. Everything should be put away in its proper place, and if you have unnecessary furnishings, get rid of them. An uncluttered house looks cleaner and more spacious. Fill in any cracks in the walls with Spackle, and repaint. Also, be sure to remove any spots from your carpet.

## 6. Put On a Good Show

Keep the following hints in mind when you have an appointment to show your home. If the weather is hot, turn on the air conditioning far enough ahead of time to cool the entire house before the prospective buyer arrives. In cool weather, the temperature inside should be comfortable, but never too hot. Put soothing music on the stereo. A fresh flower arrangement always makes a room seem special, and you can create an inviting aroma by heating cinnamon in a potpourri pot.

Put your pets outdoors, and if you have a fenced yard, it is better to send small children outside, too. You don't want the buyer to be distracted or annoyed.

Make the house look bright by opening draperies and blinds and by turning on the lights in every room. These few, simple things can make your house feel like home to a prospective buyer.

**7. Be Ready to Deal**

Do not let the sale be stopped by an offer to purchase your house at a lower price equal to only a few mortgage payments. Keep in mind that your next payments may be almost all interest. If you let a buyer get away and have to wait three months for another one, you make the next three mortgage payments. Only a few dollars of those payments will go toward the paydown of the principal.

When you decide to sell, it should be done as quickly as possible. Selling your home involves some technical aspects, so be sure you have proper professional representation.

# Money-Saving Ideas That Can Change Your Financial Direction

| Cost-Cutting Strategy | Weekly Savings |
|---|---|
| **Take your lunch** rather than buy a restaurant meal | $20-$40 |
| **Carpool to work** rather than ride alone | $30 |
| **Dine out** with the family **one less time** each week | $45 |
| **Buy one less** soft drink or cup of coffee each day | $4 |
| **Eat one less** candy bar each day | $2 |
| **Estimated Weekly Savings** | **$120** |

Saving $120 a week may sound like very little. But every little thing adds up. Doing that for thirty years will save you

 **$187,200!**

"Never Allow The Defeats Of The **Past** To Rob You Of The Victories Of The Future."

– *Robb Thompson*

# *Things To Consider Before Purchasing And Financing An Automobile*

The automobile seems to cause more people financial problems than any other item. By some unusual process, this "necessity" almost always becomes a luxury. At purchase, the buyer briefly loses control and adds costly extras. From my perspective, most automobile accidents happen on the car dealer's lot.

Because the average auto depreciates rapidly, it cannot be considered a long-term asset. It must therefore be purchased very carefully. It also must be paid for in such a way that when it wears out, enough money is available to replace it.

*VintaGe WisdOm*

— **Stanley Druckenmiller**
**U.S. Hedge Fund Manager**

**"Once you make a lot of money, it's incredibly enjoyable to give it away. It's a way to satisfy the soul."**

# 6 <u>Rules</u> for Purchasing an Automobile

***When you must buy an automobile with time payments, strictly follow these rules:***

**1. Do not use time payments to buy an "ego satisfier."** An expensive car should be yours only after your faithful financial stewardship has qualified you for it.

**2. Be sure the auto you buy suits all your transportation needs.** Don't have one sports car to transport a family of 6!

**3. Consider gasoline mileage.**

**4. Consider the warranty.** When purchasing a new vehicle, always buy the manufacturer's extended coverage. Make sure the manufacturer backs it and will pay the mechanic's bill at the dealership. If you buy a used car, choose the right dealer. Most reputable ones offer warranties. Be sure you understand the terms.

**5. If your summers are hot, buy an air conditioned car.**

**6. Ask if the dealer has any demonstrators from last year.** These usually are greatly discounted.

With these thoughts in mind, list what you need and can afford in an automobile. Remember, the right car is out there. Refuse to buy until you find it.

# 4 _Tips_ of Financing an Automobile

**_When you must buy a vehicle on time payments, several things can help pay it off much faster._**

**1. Sell your trade-in yourself.** You can get up to 25 percent more than from the dealer. If you don't sell it before you buy, trade it in for whatever the dealer will give you. When you buy, it is much more important to lower your loan amount than to get the most for your trade-in.

**2. Early payoff is a must.** It is important that the lender allow you the right to prepay your new-car loan.

**3. Always take the price discount.** No matter how low the manufacturer's interest rate, they usually will discount your new car hundreds of dollars if you pay cash.

**4. Use all available cash.** Use all trade-in and dealer-incentives money, and as much cash as you can, on your down payment. Every dollar you pay down is a dollar, plus interest, that you will not have to repay.

**Please remember:** These suggestions are subject to the approval of the manufacturer, your dealer, and the lender.

# "The Prize Is Always Greater Than The Price."

— Robb Thompson

# *8 Practical <u>Suggestions</u> For Buying Insurance*

No matter what type of insurance you need, there are several things you must consider before you buy. If you will carefully look at the following points, you will be more likely to purchase the coverage that best meets your needs. Remember, whatever you save in insurance premiums should be used to pay down your debt.

1. **Consult a financial advisor.** He will best know your individual situation and provide you with additional advice on applying the following suggestions.

2. To the best of your ability, **determine exactly how much insurance you need.** You are throwing your money down the drain when you pay for unnecessary, extra coverage.

3. **Always shop around for the best buy.** Compare different policies and prices. Investigate both what company salespeople and independent agents have to offer.

4. **Never let your agent decide what you should buy.** He will be able to give you advice, but remember, he can offer you only the coverage he sells. That may not be what you need or want.

Also, because he is paid primarily on a commission basis, he may tend to sell you more than you really need. Do not hesitate to tell one agent the price quote you received from another to see if he can give you a better deal.

**5. Always buy the highest deducible you can afford to pay.**
The purpose of insurance is to protect you from serious financial loss, not to pay for things you can easily afford yourself. The higher your deductible rate, the lower your premium will be. It is smarter to agree to pay a few small expenses out of your own pocket than to pay unreasonably high premiums.

**6. Never buy a policy you don't understand.** Your policy should be written in plain language so that you can see exactly what is covered and what is not covered.

7. Whenever possible, **make your premium payments once a year.** In most cases this will cost you less than paying semi-annually, quarterly, or monthly.

8. **Don't be afraid to investigate** a prospective insurance company. Find out if they are licensed to do business in your state. From their financial statement, determine if they are financially sound. Check with friends and other customers to see if the company promptly pays claims. Also check if they tend to adjust rates upward after a claim is filed. The agent should be able to give you the names of some customers you can call for a personal recommendation.

Every time you renew your policy, or at least once a year, re-evaluate your coverage to be sure it still meets all your needs.

## *Insurance You <u>MUST</u> Avoid*

Statistically, consumers spend about 12 percent of their disposable income on insurance. To avoid wasting valuable resources, carefully review all of your policies. Most families should have life, health (comprehensive major medical), auto, homeowner's, and disability insurance. Think twice before buying the following:

**Mortgage or Credit Life Insurance** – Buy a much-less-costly term life policy instead. Benefits remain constant.

**Car Rental Insurance** – Ask your auto insurance agent if you are already covered. And your credit card company may insure you if you rent the vehicle with their card. If you are not covered, consider the "collisions damage waiver" (CDW). Coverage costs $6-$9 a day but the security may be worth the investment.

**Automobile Medical Insurance** – If you have major medical insurance, you already are covered, and your auto liability policy covers your passengers.

**Cancer Insurance** – Adequate major medical insurance should be enough.

**Children's Life Insurance** – Generally a waste of money unless your children are the main source of family income or have a catastrophic illness. If you want the coverage, pick it up as a rider to your term policy.

**Air Travel insurance** – Your life insurance should be adequate.

**Pet Medical Insurance** – What's the chance of Rover having a catastrophic illness?

**Mugging Insurance** – Based totally on fear. A bad financial move. Use common sense when traveling.

**Contact Lens Insurance** – Expensive. Wear them carefully and put aside the money instead.

**Vacation Rain Insurance** – The people who sell this know when you buy it, they make money.

*Maximize your insurance dollar. Before buying these types of insurance, ask yourself:*

1) *Am I making this decision based on fear?*

2) *Am I covered for this need in some other policy?*

*It just makes good "CENTS."*

Now that you are well on your way
to becoming FINANCIALLY FREE...I have...

# *24 FINAL Reminders!*

Reminder #1    **Always Tithe**

Reminder #2    **Keep Your Priorities Straight**

Reminder #3    **Don't Be Double Minded**

Reminder #4    **Your Offerings Must Be Acceptable To God**

Reminder #5    **Develop Proper Understanding Of God's Wisdom**

Reminder #6    **Face Your Fears And Trust God**

Reminder #7    **Walk By Faith And Not By Sight**

Reminder #8    **Diligently Resist All Thoughts Of Poverty And Lack**

Reminder #9    **Stand In Your New Identity**

Reminder #10    **If Married, Maintain A Healthy Marriage**

Reminder #11    **Serve And Submit To Your Spiritual Leaders**

Reminder #12    **Always Walk In Love With Others**

Reminder #13    **Sow Consistently Into Good Ministries Of God**

Reminder #14    **Be Willing To Work Hard**

Reminder #15    **Keep Sin Far From Your Life**

Reminder #16    **Speak What God Says, Not Your Circumstances**

Reminder #17    **Faithfully Fulfill Your Pledges To God**

Reminder #18    **Don't Lose Sight Of God's Character**

Reminder #19    **Never Fall In Love With Money Or With Making Money**

Reminder #20    **Consistently Reach Out To The Poor**

Reminder #21    **Be A Faithful Doer Of God's Word**

Reminder #22    **Replace Your Traditional Thinking About Money**

Reminder #23    **Don't Grow Weary; Be Patient**

Reminder #24    **Remember: The Best Harvest Is Always Saved For Last**

**Dear Reader,**

Well, I hope you enjoyed the information contained in this book. I wrote this with you in mind. Now remember, <u>DON'T</u> believe that just because you read this book things will automatically change.

## Results demand action!

*Therefore, I encourage you to take 3 <u>CRITICAL</u> action steps:*

1. Ask yourself these 2 questions:
   A) What am I doing right when it comes to my finances?
   B) What must I do differently after reading this book?

2. If this book has helped you, make the decision to help someone else. Purchase another copy and give it away to someone you care about. Put the law of sowing and reaping into action.

3. Please write me your testimonies and praise reports of how God has brought you to a place of financial freedom. I want to hear how this book has helped you unlock the vault of abundance in your life.
   *(email: rt@winninginlife.org or write to: P.O. Box 558009 Chicago, IL 60655)*

# Robb Thompson

Robb Thompson is the founder and President of Robb Thompson International, an innovative company that does not just focus on developing leadership skills, but developing a leader's vision. He is also President and CEO of Robb Thompson Foundation, a 501(c)(3) organization, devoted to helping the less fortunate in the United States and other countries.

Robb's desire is to equip leaders in business and government with practical yet life-changing principles for success. His CHARACTER-CENTERED LEADERSHIP™ principles have impacted businesses, employees and leaders worldwide. Robb is a dynamic speaker and prolific author. He is known by many as one of the world's leading teachers on personal excellence and character development.

Traveling the globe speaking to more than 5000 audiences in over 40 countries, he has trained and coached business executives and mentored government leaders, including Heads of State, Cabinet Members, and Royalty. Author of more than 20 books and hundreds of personal development resources, Dr. Thompson speaks to millions of people across the earth each week through his televised broadcast, "Winning in Life."

Robb Thompson is committed to developing leaders around the world. Find out more about Robb Thompson and Robb Thompson International by visiting his website at www.robbthompson.com.

## *Robb Thompson Coaching*

**Robb Thompson Coaching** was created with you in mind! Through this dynamic program, you will experience the results you've always wanted. With personal coaching, we look to solve the three most common problems you face as a leader:

1. **Imbalance**
2. **Broken focus**
3. **Unfulfilled relationships**

As a result of going through our personal transformation system, you will walk in freedom and peace in every area of your life, you will become crystal clear about what you want and how to get there, and you'll experience fulfilling and lasting relationships.

Don't miss out on an opportunity of a lifetime. Allow RTI to assist you in achieving your dreams.

**Robb Thompson International**

18500 92nd Avenue • Tinley Park, Illinois 60487

*office* 708.614.6000 • *fax* 708.614.8288

*e-mail* coach@robbthompson.com

*web* www.robbthompson.com